Flight Test Tips & Tales from the Eye of the Examiner

Howard Fried

Column Editor for FLYING *Magazine*

McGraw-Hill

New York San Francisco Washington, D.C. Auckland Bogotá
Caracas Lisbon London Madrid Mexico City Milan
Montreal New Delhi San Juan Singapore
Sydney Tokyo Toronto

McGraw-Hill

A Division of The **McGraw·Hill** *Companies*

©1996 by **Howard Fried**.
Published by the McGraw-Hill Companies, Inc.

pbk   1 2 3 4 5 6 7 8 9 DOC/DOC 9 0 0 9 8 7 6

Library of Congress Cataloging-in-Publication Data
Fried, Howard
   Flight test tips & tales from the eye of the examiner / by Howard Fried.
      p.   cm.
   Includes index.
   ISBN 0-07-022462-5 (pbk.)
      1. Airplanes—Piloting—Examinations—Study guides. 2. Private flying—Examinations—Study guides. 3. United States. Federal Aviation Administration—Examinations—Study guides. I. Title.
TL710.F76   1996
629.132'52'076—dc20   96-25458
                                                          CIP

Acquisitions editor: Shelley IC. Chevalier
Editorial team: Susan W. Kagey, Managing Editor
               Lori Flaherty, Executive Editor
               Joann Woy, Indexer
Production team: Katherine G. Brown, Director
                Susan E. Hansford, Coding
                Wanda S. Ditch, Desktop Operator
                Linda L. King, Proofreading
                Lori L. White, Proofreading
Design team: Jaclyn J. Boone, Designer
             Katherine Lukaszewicz, Associate Designer

0224625
GEN1

This work is dedicated to Alfred M. Hunt, to whom I shall ever be grateful for recommending that I become a Designated Pilot Examiner. Al has been a true public servant in the highest sense. He is a man of integrity and honor, and, like me, is another victim of the federal bureaucracy. Mr. Hunt is a retired Federal Aviation Agency General Aviation Operations Inspector and Accident Prevention Program Manager who has devoted a major portion of his adult life to the cause of aviation safety. He has always gone the extra distance to help the airman safely occupy the airspace. Thank you, Al.

Acknowledgment

"The Violation Alternative" has been previously published in both *VSAviator* magazine and the *Journal of the Lawyer Pilots Bar Association* and is reprinted here with their gracious permission. The other appendices are previously unpublished work of mine. The "Eye of the Examiner" columns were published in *Flying* Magazine and are reprinted here with permission.

Howard J. Fried

Contents

Preface

As J. Mac McClellan, editor-in-chief of *Flying,* pointed out when he first decided to run the "Eye of the Examiner" column, "Everybody takes check rides!" More than five years ago, when I started to write the column, I set out to explain precisely how the evaluation process works in an effort to assist applicants and instructors in preparing for practical tests for various certificates and ratings.

When I was a very young lad, my mother explained to me that we learn from experience, our own and others, and that it is much less painful to learn from the experience of others. By analyzing the mistakes of previous applicants, future applicants might avoid committing the same errors. Consequently, many of the "Eye of the Examiner" columns have dealt with mistakes that applicants have made during the course of being evaluated. It is my fond hope that the column has proved helpful to aspiring aviators at all levels of training.

I have devoted the major portion of my adult life to aviation education and the certification process, and I can tell you it has been an extremely rewarding experience. There is nothing else I know of in which the teacher has the privilege of seeing as dramatic a result of his or her efforts as when instructing a primary student. Little can compare with the pleasure of issuing a certificate or rating to a well-prepared and qualified applicant. The joy expressed by successful applicants as they leave to return to their instructors with their new certificates in hand is a wonder to behold; it is a gratifying experience indeed for the evaluator. And to think the examiner gets paid for this!

The "Eye of the Examiner" column is certainly very controversial, as demonstrated by the amount and nature of the mail it generates. It seems someone out there is just waiting to jump on anything I write and take violent exception to almost any statement I make. I have a huge file of what I am pleased to call my hate mail. Of approximately equal size is the file of favorable mail, my fan mail. The editors of *Flying* forward to me all the mail relating to the "Eye of the Examiner" column, and almost every one gets a personal answer. In fact, the only ones that don't get answered are those that object to something I wrote merely for the sake of objecting without making a valid point of any kind, those with an illegible or no return address, and, of course, the anonymous ones.

I think it is safe to assume that every airman (or to be politically correct, every airperson) is vitally interested in the evaluation process and the procedures by which it is accomplished. Hopefully, this compilation of "Eye" columns will strip away some of the mystery surrounding the flight tests that we all face from time to time.

Here, then, is a selected group of "Eye" columns. It is my hope that it will prove not only instructive but entertaining. If I have been successful, it will be both.

Howard J. Fried

Introduction

All applicants show up for a flight test with some degree of "checkitis" or exam jitters, which presents the examiner with a problem. The examiner wants to see the applicant's best effort, and he or she certainly can't see that if the applicant is all tied up in knots. Some applicants are so uptight they are utterly incapable of expressing themselves. In one extreme case, a private applicant, a young medical doctor, showed up for his test with such a case of nerves that he had to excuse himself and go to the gentlemen's lounge to toss his cookies prior to the start of the check ride! I helped him over his nervous condition by engaging in the following conversation:

Me: Let's see now, you had four years of undergraduate college work, four years of medical school, and I don't know how much internship and residency before taking your state boards. Is that correct?

Applicant: Sure is.

Me: Were you this nervous and uptight when you took those state boards to practice medicine after all that time, study, and money?

Applicant: No.

Me: Then why be so concerned about such a simple little thing as a private pilot flight test?

Applicant: Well, put that way......

Me: Let me ask you another question, OK?

Applicant: Go ahead.

Me: Today is November 7, 1986. On November 7, 1996, is it going to make any difference whether you received your Private Pilot Certificate on November 7, 1986, or November 9 or 10, 1986?

Applicant: Well, when you put it that way, I suppose not.

Once we got that over with, he settled down and performed very well.

Putting an applicant at ease can be very difficult. Some examiners are better at it than others. And some applicants just can't seem to relax. As the following story shows, there's more than one side to every story.

Not too long ago, I received a letter from a reader describing what he referred to as "the check ride from hell." This letter was in response to an "Eye of the Examiner" column in which I had discussed the strange situation of those applicants who had completed their training and been recommended but for one reason or another never took the final test. This writer listed all the things he believed his examiner had done wrong that led to him busting his ride and refusing to return for a retest, even with a different examiner. Some of the applicant's complaints are quite subjective (open to interpretation) and impossible to evaluate, some stretch the limits of the standards of the Practical Test Standards (PTS), and some clearly reach beyond the PTS.

In his original letter, my reader didn't say what kind of airplane he used for the flight test, but he did say that the examiner had him involved in "inverted maneuvers." If the test was conducted in any of the common training aircraft, I very much doubt that they were in truly inverted flight at any time, but if they were, it is far outside what the PTS requires. This complaint is probably based on a misperception on the part of the applicant. If, however the maneuver was violent enough to cause the applicant to believe they were inverted, it was no doubt outside the limits of the PTS.

My reader complained that the examiner required him to do 45-degree-banked, 360-degree turns under the hood. The only time I had to do this was on my ATP (air transport pilot) flight test, and while I suppose the examiner could claim this maneuver falls under the heading "unusual attitudes" with a view-limiting device in place, I'm sure that is not what the FAA had in mind when the private pilot practical test was designed. My correspondent and his instructor both quoted the examiner as asserting that he knew this was not in the PTS, but he requires it anyway "for the safety of the applicant." They quoted him as having told the FAA that this maneuver should be included in the PTS and that he requires it of all his applicants.

On the oral portion of the practical test, which had occurred some three weeks earlier, my correspondent stated that the examiner had found fault with the POH (Pilots Operating Handbook) for the airplane, claiming that he wrote them better. He also found fault with FAA publications, according to both the writer and his instructor.

The reader described his examiner in terms that can only be defined as overbearing. He described the examiner's attitude as "extreme arrogance and egotism from a 30,000-hour WWII veteran and designated examiner." The correspondent went on to say that the examiner "grabs (the) yoke on downwind and turns to base as a twin is on final, almost causing a midair." According to the applicant, the examiner claimed the local (tower) controller didn't know where the traffic was.

The writer also said the examiner told him that he had three chances to land on the selected spot and the first one didn't count. Please note: The FAA says in no uncertain terms, "No second chances! The applicant must get each TASK right the first time, or he fails the maneuver and thus the complete test." The writer went on to say that he aced the first landing (the one that didn't count), but that he was so upset by then that he blew the other two.

I am reluctant to criticize any designated pilot examiner, but in this case I wonder if the examiner couldn't have treated the applicant with more (or even some degree of) respect. I know of two examiners who lost their designations for imposing their own standards rather than those of the PTS, plus one who was severely criticized for doing so. My reader said he complained, in writing, to the local FSDO about this adventure, but as of the date of this writing he had no reply, although the FAA is required to answer all written complaints.

This applicant's letter so intrigued me that I began to delve a little deeper into the situation. I interviewed, by telephone, the applicant, his instructor, and, finally, the examiner who administered the check ride.

I learned from the applicant that the airplane involved was a Cherokee Warrior (PA28-151 or 161). I also learned that the applicant, who originally called himself a drop-out, does intend to retake the examination at a future date (with a different examiner).

The recommending instructor who had trained the applicant is a former Marine Corps pilot and an experienced CFI. He said he talked with the examiner between the time the applicant had his oral portion of the practical test and the flight portion and then again after the applicant returned from the check ride. He backed up the applicant's story regarding the attitude of the examiner and his insistence on testing some specific maneuvers not included in the published standards of the PTS. The flight instructor also understandably insisted that he will never again expose an applicant of his to that particular examiner.

Far be it from me to justify or excuse inappropriate action by a designated pilot examiner, but when I interviewed the examiner himself, a somewhat different story began to emerge. He claimed he always attempts to relax all his applicants. Obviously, in this instance, he failed to do so. I know from personal experience that this can be an extremely difficult undertaking. In spite of the best efforts of the examiner, some applicants remain tense and uptight throughout the entire examination.

As I indicated, the applicant's statement regarding an "inverted maneuver" was no doubt based on a misperception on his part. A Warrior simply cannot sustain true inverted flight, and a relatively inexperienced pilot might very well perceive a wingover to be an "inverted maneuver." However, such violent maneuvering is not an approved activity for an examiner who is conducting a private flight test.

As far as taking control and cutting off the twin on final and then being required to take evasive action is concerned, if the controller didn't make a big deal of it, it could also be explained by the different perceptions of a highly experienced pilot as opposed to those of a nervous student.

Finally, many, if not most, examiners have certain things that they emphasize in an effort to make sure they are turning safe pilots loose in the airspace. Some examiners, in an effort to illustrate a point, will demonstrate or have the applicant perform a maneuver that might not be on the PTS. When an examiner does this, he or she should make it very clear that this activity is not part of the test, and the applicant won't fail if his or her performance is unsatisfactory on this maneuver. In fact, this sort of activity is usually more in the nature of a demonstration by the examiner than a task for the applicant. The examiner in this instance assured me that he followed this procedure. If he did tell the applicant that the two 360s under the hood with a 45-degree bank would not be counted, perhaps the applicant was so upset that he simply failed to hear the examiner's explanation. This is no doubt something we'll never know for sure.

There you have it. Both sides of the story of "the check ride from hell." Although it is quite possible that either one is right, it is equally possible that they are both right.

"Eye of the Examiner" Columns

1

One of the common "tricks" some examiners use to "catch" the unwary applicant is to board the aircraft and sit on the lap belt without fastening it. The examiner waits for the applicant (the pilot-in-command) to notice he's not buckled up, as well as to administer complete passenger briefing. This the applicant frequently fails to do—despite the fact that he goes through the checklist, including the admonishment to adjust seats and fasten belts, out loud.

After arriving at the run-up pad and completing the pretakeoff checklist, the following conversation takes place:

Examiner: You ready?
Applicant: Yes.
E: You sure?
A: Yes.
E: Check everything on the checklist, did you?
A: Yes.
E: Go back to the very beginning of the checklist and check again.
A: Okay. (Rereads list.) All done.
E: Who is responsible for this flight?
A: I am.
E: How about item one (or two, as the case may be)?
A: [Abashed] You better buckle up?

This scenario occurs again and again, and what it demonstrates is that many applicants run through the checklist in a very perfunctory manner. If this is the way a checklist is treated in the test situation, one wonders just how that person will run his checks when he is out on his own, with inexperienced passengers.

In each of the Practical Test Standards, the examiner is required to evaluate the applicant's use of the checklist, and ofttimes he sees the applicant pay lip service to the list, merely going through the motions of using it; this applies to all phases of the flight. After completing the run-up and performing the takeoff, chances are the applicant never consults a checklist again (en route, emergency, prelanding, landing or shutdown) throughout the duration of the check ride.

An applicant can get himself in trouble right from the start, with the go/no-go decision. If he opts to go when the weather dictates that he could not legally complete the test (ceiling too low to achieve sufficient altitude to do the stalls and recover), he could fail the test for poor judgment; at the very least, the examiner would be put in the position of having to make the applicant's decision for him—creating a negative first impression that will carry over to the actual check ride.

These are just two examples of the kind of thoughtless things an examiner sees applicants do. Often the problem is simply that the applicant is not used to thinking of himself as the pilot-in-command.

This is particularly evident in the case of the private applicant, for up until this time, whenever he (or she) has been in an airplane in the driver's seat, if there was anyone else aboard it was an instructor. The applicant/student could turn to his right for advice and instruction. Now, on the check ride, it's a whole new ballgame.

Throughout the entire test, the examiner doesn't want to hear any question that starts out, "Do you want . . . ?" It's not about what the examiner wants, but rather what the FAA requires as set forth in the Practical Test Standards. Every examiner, whenever he calls for a maneuver, frequently hears, "How do you want . . . ?" Again, it's not about how the examiner wants it done; the examiner's status throughout the test is "passenger/observer" and his function is merely to observe and evaluate the applicant's performance.

After landing, the examiner may use another "trick." He may suggest to the applicant that he be let out of the aircraft to go into the office and start the paperwork while the applicant returns the airplane to the tie-down and secures it. At least 50 percent of applicants will let the examiner dismount from the aircraft *with the engine running!* This, of course, is a big no-no. No one should ever be permitted to leave an airplane without the engine being shut down and the ignition turned off. Again, if an applicant will do this with an examiner in the test situation, is he not likely to do the same thing as a private pilot, perhaps with young children aboard?

It is beyond comprehension for an applicant to present himself to an examiner for a flight test without ever having seen or been exposed to the appropriate Practical Test Standards, but it happens all too often. Since the government does student aviators an enormous favor by providing them with a list of very specific standards, spelled out in excruciating detail, along with the procedures and techniques by which these standards may be met, it only makes good sense to take advantage of this generous offer. When this is thoroughly understood, then—and only then—can the applicant begin to take command and assume the mantle of responsibility that goes with the decision-making process.

30 August 1991

Dear Editor,

I have been a *Flying* reader since I was about 12 years old. I bought my first issue in 1965, and have saved it and almost every other issue since.

I am a student pilot, have 50 hours and will be finishing my private and attending A&P school in Arizona. This will constitute a career change for me. I have been a civilian and military policeman for 17 years.

Now, I am not sure where your magazine found this new writer, Howard J. Fried, but I hope you do not keep him long.

I may not have much aviation experience, but law experience I do have. Your magazine reported on the crash of a Learjet some years ago. In that article it was clearly reported that the United States Supreme Court did make clear case law that a flight examiner is the PILOT-IN-COMMAND, not the examinee.

On top of Mr. Fried's article (to the best of knowledge) being incorrect, I also found his little tricks that substitute for an examination of skill and responsibility to be offensive. I pray that he is not the best the FAA examiner system has to offer. I have trained trainee police officers and would never do this type of outright garbage to them. Our lives are at stake when we go out on watch, just like when I go up in an aircraft.

If this is what the FAA calls an examiner, then it is no wonder the general aviation sector has a problem.

Signed

W.C.P.

September 9, 1991

Dear Mr. P_____:

The editors of *Flying* have forwarded a copy of your letter regarding my September column to me, and I feel compelled to answer it personally.

I certainly hope the editors do keep me around for a long time—I really need the money!

Seriously, though, with respect to who is PIC on a flight test, I refer you to FAR 61.47, which clearly places command authority on the applicant, absent agreement to the contrary, or unless the situation requires that the examiner act as PIC (for example an instrument flight test in actual IMC).

Mr. P_____, if you think I'm looking for "gotchas" to nail an applicant for any little deviation from the standard when I administer a flight test, then you are missing the point altogether. On the other hand, if you realize the importance of impressing on the applicant the frightening responsibility attached to being in command of an airplane with passengers aboard, then you must recognize the validity of the techniques mentioned.

Perhaps if we'd used the term "techniques" rather than "tricks" you might have interpreted the entire column in a different, more favorable light.

Good luck in your new career (aviation). Obviously, you are a keen aviation student, and the industry can always use thinking people.

Sincerely,

Howard J. Fried

Dear Sir:

About the September 1991 article by Howard J. Fried. I do not agree and I'm pretty sure that the FAA does not condone using tricks to fool an applicant on a check ride. The FAA never mentioned "tricks" in any examiner training course that I have attended. The FAA already has a bad reputation without accusing them of using tricks. "Tricks" should be left out of the check ride!

There are enough different objectives for each task on a flight test for an applicant to fail without making any tricks up.

I do agree with Howard that all applicants should have a working knowledge of the appropriate Practical Test Standards for their particular test.

Come on Howard, lighten up!

Sincerely,

R.W.C.
FAA Designated Examiner

2

Commercial applicants are now required to demonstrate competence in the performance of a maneuver that most of today's flight instructors didn't have to learn as commercial students, or even as flight instructor applicants. Since the reintroduction of 8s on pylons into the commercial curriculum, we are confronted with a situation in which an entire generation of instructors are attempting to teach something they never had to learn, and most of them are doing it wrong.

The on-pylon 8, done properly, is no doubt the most difficult maneuver in the commercial curriculum, but it is also the most gratifying when it is done right. What the modern flight instructor seems to fail to understand is that the pivotal altitude is critical within *inches*. There is only one very precise altitude at which the extension of the lateral axis of the aircraft will appear to pivot around a spot at ground level at a very precise groundspeed.

In the performance of this maneuver we frequently see one or both of two serious errors. One: The applicant attempts to use the wingtip as the sight line for pivoting around the point (pylon), and two: He uses a large, tall structure as the "pylon" around which this line of sight (from the wingtip) rotates as the airplane circles the object.

In the first instance, it is *not* the wingtip, but rather the lateral axis of the airplane, that will pivot about the pylon at a given groundspeed, and this lateral axis does not run from wingtip to wingtip. What the lateral axis does is bisect the airplane through the center of gravity from side to side. Establish stable, straight-and-level flight and observe where the horizon cuts the side windows of the airplane: *This* is the lateral axis, and an imaginary line extended from this point to the ground is the line of sight that, at the critical pivotal altitude, will cause the pylon (point at ground level) to stand still while the airplane rotates (circles) around it.

Secondly, since the pivotal altitude is extremely precise (within inches, remember), the pylon must be selected with care. It must be a specific point at ground level, such as the base of a telephone pole where it enters the ground, the base of a tree or bush at ground level, or some similar object.

Now, since there is one very precise groundspeed at which the extension of the lateral axis will cause the airplane to pivot about the pylon, the pilot must vary his altitude as his groundspeed varies due to wind effect—the slower the lower, the faster the higher.

Instead, what the examiner frequently sees when he calls for on-pylon 8s is the applicant attempting to pivot about a large object such as a barn or silo by holding the wingtip of the airplane somewhere on the object.

Somehow, the current crop of flight instructors must be themselves educated so that they can teach this maneuver properly. Then the examiner won't have to disapprove the applicant's application or interrupt the flight test and demonstrate the correct way to perform the maneuver.

3

An interesting phenomenon, observed by virtually all pilot examiners, is the extreme single-mindedness of most applicants when placed in the test situation. We often see an applicant make a plan and then stick to it as though there were no other way to accomplish the objective, despite the fact that conditions make it impossible to complete the task as planned.

For example, an applicant for a private pilot certificate plans a cross-country flight at an altitude of 4,500 feet, based on the weather briefing he received from the flight service specialist; but when he starts the flight, he encounters a broken ceiling at 3,000 feet. Ignoring the fact that he will be in violation of the cloud-separation rule as soon as he climbs within 500 feet of the cloud layer, the applicant plunges ahead, aiming right for the cloud. When asked what he has in mind, he replies, "I've made my trip plan for 4,500 feet, and I've been taught to always follow my plan."

An examiner I know always arranges, on the initial takeoff of a private or commercial check ride, to use a runway that requires crosswind technique on the part of the applicant and then calls for a soft-field takeoff. Time and again (certainly more often than not), he sees the applicant concentrate so hard on getting the nosewheel up out of the hypothetical mud and applying perfect soft-field technique that he ignores the crosswind and lifts off gently drifting off the runway. It's another example of applicant single-mindedness.

These two cases demonstrate slightly different problems that inexperienced pilots have. The first is an example of inflexibility, while the second illustrates the inability of the inexperienced pilot to focus on two tasks simultaneously. Certainly, any competent pilot should be able to combine soft-field technique with the application of crosswind correction to take off; certainly, a pilot should be prepared to adjust his thinking and alter his plan to meet changing conditions. But in the test situation, we rarely see either of these reactions on the part of the applicant.

These kinds of shortsightedness make it very difficult for a pilot to work well in a busy traffic pattern, where several airplanes with different performance capability are all arriving at more or less the same time. If the pilot has always flown the pattern at exactly the same distance out and at exactly the same altitude and speed, what will he be able to do when the controller says, "Extend your downwind, please" or "Make short approach, cleared to land?" In an ideal world, conditions of wind, weather, and traffic would always be perfect, and we could consistently do everything exactly the same way every time. But in the real world, that's not the way it works, and perhaps it's a good thing—for therein lies the challenge of flight. We must be flexible and stand ready to adapt to conditions as we find them, rather than rigidly stick to a plan that, although perfectly fine when made, is no longer applicable.

4

The FAA assumes the posture that an applicant for a flight test can do no wrong: Whatever he or she does is the responsibility of the recommending instructor. If an applicant is properly prepared, there is no excuse for him to bust a check ride, and it is up to the flight instructor to get 'em properly prepared! Bearing this in mind, it is a constant source of wonder how many applicants show up for check rides totally inadequately prepared. Of course, it makes a great impression on the examiner when the applicant arrives some 30 or more minutes late for a flight-test appointment, an event that happens with some frequency.

Then there's the applicant (believe it or not, this has actually happened on more than one occasion) who shows up for his check ride without an application for his certificate or rating. When asked for the application, the response is, "What application? My instructor told me all I need is his endorsement in my logbook!" Can you believe this? Just think: An instructor who had to have executed a minimum of four (and probably more) 8710 Application for Certificate or Rating forms himself for his own private, commercial, instrument, and instructor certificates and ratings tells a trainee of his own that such an application is unnecessary. And then instead of being embarrassed, the instructor is resentful of the fact that the examiner sends the applicant back (without a disapproval notice/pink slip) to get a properly executed application! This, of course, necessitates the making of a new appointment, leaving a hole in the examiner's no-doubt busy schedule.

The frequency with which private applicants show up for flight tests without a view-limiting device (hood or foggles) is absolutely appalling. My own policy when this happens is as follows: When we get to the airplane and are ready to fly, if I notice the absence of a hood I make a snide remark such as, "What are you going to do when I ask you to put on a hood?" The applicant may then say "What hood? Who needs a hood?" and I point out that the Practical Test Standard calls for some instrument work. In any event, at this time I offer to lend the applicant a hood or foggles, whichever he is used to using. But if I fail to notice the absence of a hood, and we actually get in the air, and I ask the applicant to put on his hood and he hasn't got one with him, he fails the check ride and goes home with a pinkie. This, of course, does embarrass the instructor.

Then there are the numerous applicants who present themselves for the flight test without the required endorsements or who have failed to meet the experience requirement for the certificate or rating for which they are applying. This failure to meet the experience requirement usually takes the form of the private applicant who reports no instrument time on his application or who shows inadequate night experience. I've also had pilot applicants show up with less than the required cross-country experience, or with cross-country flights logged that failed to meet the minimum distance requirement.

Some applicants bring a legally unairworthy airplane for the check ride (out of annual or some such discrepancy). If an instrument flight test is involved, and the airplane is not currently certified for instrument flight (altimeter and static system check and the like), the ride can go forth, but it must all be accomplished in simulated conditions and not in the system. By the bye, an instrument applicant once came in for his certification flight test without a view-limiting device.

These are just a few examples of the lack of preparation that every examiner sees in the course of a year or two of administering flight tests. There are many others, but these should suffice to wake up any instructor or applicant who reads this to the fact that a bit more care and attention to detail would make the examiner's task infinitely easier and more enjoyable and save the instructor's record from unnecessary busts and the applicant unnecessary expense.

5

Applicants for flight tests consistently demonstrate a lack of understanding of the privileges and limitations of the certificate or rating for which they are applying. And this is by no means limited to the private applicant. In fact, it is most apparent in the case of the commercial applicant, who believes either that he has the unlimited ability to fly for hire or that he can do almost nothing by way of being an aviator for pay.

Most applicants (for all certificates or ratings) completely forget about the necessity of completing a biennial flight review when asked what they have to do to maintain the privileges of the rating for which they are applying. Many private applicants are under the misapprehension that they must have made at least three takeoffs and landings within the past 90 days in order to be current to fly an airplane, failing to relate this requirement to the privilege of carrying passengers. Who knows how they expect to get the three takeoffs and landings in—perhaps with an instructor? Then, of course, there is the large group of private applicants who believe that if they are current for carrying passengers at night they must still do three in the day, and that the day landings must be touch-and-goes.

Applicants seeking an additional aircraft rating frequently fail to relate passenger-carrying currency to category and class of aircraft, mistakenly believing that currency in a more complex aircraft will cover a less complex or simpler one, that is, if you are current in a multiengine airplane, you're automatically covered in a single. Of course this is not so. An individual must be current in category and class both day and night, and the more ratings an individual acquires, the more carefully he or she must watch to make sure that all requirements are met prior to charging off into the blue with anyone else aboard. By the same token, many applicants labor under the misapprehension that they must be current in type, that is, make and model, not realizing that if they are current for carrying passengers in a Baron, they can legally carry people in (for example) a Cessna 310 or a Piper Seneca, but that unless they have also made three takeoffs and landings in the past 90 days in a single-engine airplane, they cannot legally carry passengers in a single.

Instrument-rating applicants frequently fail to thoroughly understand the six, six, and six requirement for currency for operating in the instrument system or in IMC (instrument meteorological conditions). They all seem to know that to be current for instrument flight they must have six hours of instrument flight (either actual or simulated) within the last six months and must have executed six instrument approaches within that six-month period. They also seem to know that three of the hours must be in the same category of aircraft as that for which they are seeking to maintain currency. What many of them *don't* seem to know is what a category of aircraft is, often confusing category with class, or even with type.

Also, they all seem to know that they have six months after their currency expires to get themselves current with a view-limiting device and a safety pilot before they are required to take an instrument competency check with a "double-eye" (instrument instructor). What they often fail to realize is that during this latter six-month period they may not either, one, file and get in the system, or two, fly in the clouds (IMC). They cannot do this because they are, temporarily at least, not instrument rated, and if the safety pilot is, the currency seeker may not log the time (or approaches), for the safety pilot is then required to act as PIC (pilot-in-command) and only he can log the time.

The foregoing are just a few of the many misconceptions examiners observe when quizzing applicants regarding the privileges and limitations of the certificate or rating for which they are applying.

6

Every pilot shows up for a check ride with some degree or another of checkitis. Checkitis goes by many different names, among which are "exam jitters" and "butterflies in the stomach." But whatever it is called, it poses a problem for the examiner because he wants to see the applicant's best effort, which certainly can't be shown by an applicant who is all tied up in knots.

All examiners, some more than others, make an effort to calm down the applicant, and the degree of success in this calming-down process will have a direct bearing on the outcome.

On the other hand, this heightened state of nerves, if properly controlled, can be put to work to the advantage of the applicant. Personally, I've been taking check rides all my life (at least two and sometimes as many as five per year for well over 20 years), all with FAA inspectors, and I psych myself up each time by telling myself, "I'm going to show the man how I fly, and if it's not good enough, I don't deserve to pass!" It seems that when I force myself to believe this (emotionally as well as intellectually), I relax and give the inspector a good ride. I have busted a ride or two, and in each case, I knew exactly what I did wrong and when. Believe it or not, it didn't bother me to bust, because I knew how I goofed. I just went back a day or two later and did that part again.

Here's a tip for passing a flight test, any flight test: Give the examiner letter-perfect answers in the oral exam phase of the check. If you really know your stuff and come out with crisp, clear, accurate answers to each of the examiner's questions (without hesitating), he will be impressed to the extent that when you get to the airplane, if you give him a marginal performance (perhaps slightly exceeding the tolerances), he will be making excuses for you (perhaps a gust did it). He knows it can't be your fault—after all, you really proved you know your stuff during the oral exam, and he's already decided that you are good, so in order to put you down, he has to question his own judgment. On the other hand, if you do a marginal, barely pass-able job on the oral quizzing, the examiner has already decided that you can't be any good in the airplane, and sure enough one little goof on your part will confirm his judgment that you really should be sent back for more instruction. No one likes to question his own judg-ment, so if we give him a perfect performance during the oral exam, we are making it easy for him to pass us.

Remember, the examiner wants to pass every applicant who comes to him, and that makes three of you at least: You want to pass, your instructor wants you to pass, and the examiner wants you to pass. From the examiner's viewpoint, it's a lot easier to pass an ap-plicant than to issue a pink slip. There's a lot more paperwork in-volved, not to mention the fact that he has to get back in the airplane with the applicant at some future date and do at least part of the check ride over again. I'd like to see every applicant meet the stan-dard and pass his flight test, but unfortunately it doesn't always work out that way, and occasionally one shows up for a check ride who isn't quite prepared, and he has to go back for additional instruction.

7

Not only is a thorough knowledge of the airspace regulations required by the FAA, but it's also just plain good sense for the applicant to know these regulations in order to avoid unsafe practices or procedures, or at the very least, to avoid committing a violation. Therefore, virtually all pilot examiners devote a portion of the oral quiz to this subject. Personally, I do this as part of the assignment of a cross-country plan on the private pilot flight test.

The technique I use to bring out the applicant's knowledge of the airspace regulations is to ask the applicant to plan a trip, in full compliance with all applicable FARs, to a destination that has a control zone, but no airport traffic area. This gives me a chance to quiz the applicant on the difference between these two commonly confused kinds of controlled airspace. I also select a destination to which a direct route takes us through a TCA (fortunately we live where this is possible). This provides me with the opportunity to see just what the applicant will do about the TCA. Surprisingly, a great many private applicants will plan a route by which they give the outer limit of the TCA a wide berth, apparently not realizing that if they wish to avoid the TCA they can duck under most of it. When I ask why they don't take a more direct route, I'm often told, "My instructor told me to stay away from there. It's reserved for big airplanes only."

I used to greet the applicant, and after putting him or her at ease (hopefully), I would tell him how much I weigh, and ask him to plan a trip. However, several years ago an FAA inspector suggested that I ask the applicant to plan the trip in full compliance with all the FARs and wait to see if my weight is asked. If not—and it usually isn't—when we get to the required documents on the airplane and the applicant tells me that it must have an equipment list with sufficient data to work a weight-and-balance aboard, I can express surprise that he didn't ask my weight. I then have him work a weight-and-balance for our trip, and more often than not, he will do so using a hypothetical weight and center of gravity from a sample problem rather than the actual data for the airplane we will be using. Of course, this is unacceptable, so we do it over, using the real data. We then discuss the effect of being out of the envelope (overgross or out of center-of-gravity limits fore or aft).

Our trip plan will take us through, over, or around an ARSA, and we discuss ARSA requirements. I then point to a TRSA on the chart and ask for a one-word answer to the question, "What do you have to do about a TRSA?" The answer, of course, is "Nothing."

When assigning the trip plan, I advise the applicant that we will lay over at our airport of first intended landing until 10 p.m., then proceed to a second destination. For this second destination I select an airport that has a beacon but pilot-operated lighting for runway lights. What I'm looking for, of course, is to see if the applicant has the smarts to look this up and note on his trip log the fact that he must key his mike a given number of times on a given frequency. If he doesn't do this, and most don't, when we discuss his planning, I ask him if this airport has lights. Observing the symbol for a beacon and the letter "L" on the chart, he says, "Yes, it has lights." I then ask if they're going to be on. He then wakes up to the fact that he should have looked it up, and I get to make some snide remark about how 10:45 p.m. tonight when you're 10 miles out is no time to be sitting there with a flashlight in your mouth while you're flipping the pages of the *Airport Facility Directory* with both hands and the airplane is going into a dance.

These are just a few of the kinds of things an examiner, if he's good, will do on the oral portion of the flight test to force an applicant to THINK, which is what a good instructor wants you to be able to do.

8

Virtually none of us would dream of turning an automobile into an intersection without looking carefully both ways to see if another car is coming, yet a great many pilots enter a turn in an airplane without so much as a glance outside. I have previously discussed the single-mindedness of most applicants who are being observed by pilot examiners, and this condition sometimes extends to a failure to clear the area prior to engaging in some maneuver in which there is a potential loss of altitude.

When the examiner calls for a stall, flight at minimum controllable airspeed, or some such maneuver, the applicant apparently becomes so engrossed in attempting to perform the maneuver properly that he may forget to look around the sky while flying the maneuver. Some pilots even neglect to clear the area by making a turn of at least 90 degrees in each direction so no potentially conflicting traffic can hide behind a wing or under the nose. Your instructor reminded you to clear the area before beginning a maneuver, and that's good. Your examiner expects you to remember.

Back in the days when the primary training airplanes were the J-3 Cub and the 7AC Champ, I saw much better airmen in terms of their ability to smoothly manipulate the controls and maneuver an airplane around in the sky. However, since the training wheel moved to the front of the airplane, pilots can get away with a pretty sloppy job of flying without fear of a ground loop, and they do. With the increasing sophistication of both the equipment we fly and the environment (airspace) in which we operate, it is literally amazing that anyone can learn the vast amount of material required of a private pilot. Some part of a new pilot's flying education has to suffer, and often it is surveillance of the skies around him. He is too busy paying attention to the internal cockpit chores.

Why anyone would discard a 25,000-mile reference (nature's horizon) and replace it with a three-and-one-half-inch reference (the artificial gyro horizon) when he doesn't have to is beyond me, but a great many private and commercial applicants do just that by focusing nearly all of their attention on the instrument panel. As a result, their flying is very imprecise. Worse yet, if an applicant fails to maintain adequate surveillance of the airspace around him, and if he fails to properly clear the area prior to any maneuver in which his vision will be blocked or in which there is a potential loss of altitude, it is a downer and the examiner has no discretion whatever—it's an automatic "pinkie."

Of course in VMC (visual meteorological conditions), we are all responsible for seeing and avoiding other traffic whether or not we are in contact with ATC or even when we are on an IFR clearance, but many of today's pilots fail to scan the skies as they are supposed (even required) to do. Again, I think this is doubtless a result of having all those fabulous goodies on the panels in front of them. They become so engrossed with playing with all the toys (loran, RNAV, and so forth) that they sometimes forget to look out the window.

If an applicant keeps his head inside the cockpit on a flight test, I have no choice. He fails the check ride and has to go back and face his instructor. If an applicant exceeds the tolerance a little on some required maneuver or another, the examiner has a degree of discretion. I can counsel the applicant and hope he remembers his minor mistake, or I can issue a disapproval notice (pink slip) and guarantee that the applicant will remember the mistake. The only question in my mind is whether or not I must impose the memory guarantee. However, when an applicant fails to clear the area when safety requires it or fails to keep looking around outside the airplane, the FAA gives me no choice. I must issue the pink slip disapproval notice. The moral of this story is, keep a careful watch for traffic on all flights, including your check ride.

9

Regardless of the certificate or rating sought, everybody wants to pass his or her check ride, but very few applicants are looking for a gift. In other words, most applicants don't want Santa Claus for an examiner. Of course, neither do they want Mephistopheles, who will, pass or fail, give the pilot a hard time on the flight test. The test situation is not necessarily supposed to be a pleasant experience, but neither is it required to be particularly unpleasant.

The point here is that the vast majority of applicants want to be thoroughly tested to the standard of the PTS (Practical Test Standard). They want a thorough check ride for their own sense of well-being. In order to have confidence to fly as pilot-in-command, we all need to know that an impartial expert has looked us over and found us qualified.

Although the check ride is not supposed to be an educational experience, most applicants come away from the flight test having learned quite a bit. Of course, if the examiner is found to be deliberately teaching during the course of the check ride when he should merely be evaluating the applicant's knowledge and skill, the FAA will counsel the examiner, and if this practice of teaching instead of evaluating persists, the examiner will likely lose his designation. In other words, the applicant may very well come away from the check ride feeling that he has learned from the experience, but not from the examiner.

Personally, I've been taking check rides all my life, and I've learned something new each time. If every applicant will only approach the flight test with an open mind and in a receptive mood, he is sure to come away enriched. Remember, if the applicant fails to pass the check ride, it's no disgrace; the failure reflects on the recommending instructor, not the applicant.

After testing several examples of a given instructor's product, I begin to get an idea of the quality of the instructor's teaching. It takes several tests of an instructor's students to form an opinion, because on any given check ride, the student will make the instructor look good or bad. An instructor can pour his heart and soul into the training of a particularly difficult student, and finally just give up and say, "There's nothing more I can do for this person. I'll send him in and if he has a good day, he might pass." After the flight test (pass or fail), the examiner says to himself, "Boy, this one had lousy training," when, in reality, he had the best there is. On the other hand, there's the instructor who views his job as simply sitting in the right seat of the airplane and preventing the applicant from committing suicide while he teaches himself how to fly. Along comes the natural who studies hard, does everything right, and unassisted learns to fly. He takes his check ride and impresses the examiner to the extent that the examiner says to himself, "Boy, this guy had a great instructor." See what I mean? The student can make the instructor look good or bad, but after seeing half a dozen of his or her students, the examiner can pretty well tell the quality of teaching offered by that instructor.

10

Today, as I write this, it is the next-to-the-last day of the month, and it's happened again (as it does once or twice a year to all pilot examiners): I got a call from the chief instructor at a local flight school who wanted to schedule a flight test. And the test must be today or tomorrow, for the applicant's written result expires at midnight on the last day of the month. Here's an applicant who has had up to 25 months from the time he passed his written examination— which attests to the fact that he has met the knowledge requirement for his certificate or rating—and now, all at once, panicsville: He has two days to meet the skill requirement for an examiner.

What frequently happens in these cases is that the applicant, full of excuses for the delay ("I was sick for a month," "I lost my job and didn't get a new one for a month," "I moved," and so forth), pressures an instructor into recommending him when he isn't really ready and then attempts to pressure an examiner into passing him on his check ride when he really shouldn't be passed. Sometimes he will even attempt to talk the examiner into retrodating the paperwork to indicate that the test was timely, when in fact it wasn't. In these cases the answer is a resounding "No." All the applicant (or instructor) who makes such a request has accomplished is to lower himself in the esteem of the examiner.

It is now two days later. In an effort to accommodate the applicant, I squeezed him into my schedule for today, and he did show up for his ride. However, he didn't have his written result with him, his application wasn't signed by either himself or his instructor, and he didn't have the airplane paperwork. Since the school where he was trained is on the same airport where I operate, I sent him back for all this stuff. When he came back a few minutes later with everything in hand, we started to go over his application, and guess what? He showed only 11 hours of solo time. When I pointed out that the regulations (he was a Part 61 applicant) require 20, he informed me that his instructor (who had by now signed his application) had informed him that he only needed 10 hours of solo cross-country experience. I showed him the regulations regarding private pilot experience requirements and sent him away. After he retakes the written exam and finishes his training, I will see him again.

On the other hand, one of the most gratifying experiences of my entire life, and certainly the most satisfying as an examiner, came under similar circumstances. This time the applicant was an 83-year-old man who came for his instrument check ride. He had already failed with another examiner (a friend of mine) who sent Mr. Silver to me for his recheck because that examiner's schedule was full, and Mr. Silver had to get the ride in before his written expired at midnight.

Despite the fact that Mr. Silver had 800 hours of instrument dual instruction (that's right—not a misprint, 800 hours), I had to turn him down again. He didn't hear any of the ATC radio calls, even his approach clearances. I told him that I knew his hearing was okay (he had a valid medical certificate). Obviously he was concentrating so hard on flying the airplane that he just shut everything else out.

With grim determination he advised me that he was going to attend a weekend cram course and retake the instrument written. (The course was being offered in a city 250 miles away, starting the next day.) I loaned him an aircraft band radio and suggested that he tune approach control and follow all the calls to and from a specific aircraft, and when that one is handed off, pick up another and follow it through, ad infinitum. He thanked me and said he would see me in 30 days with a new recommendation.

Sure enough, 30 days later Mr. Silver showed up, returned my radio, and scheduled another check ride. This time he did everything right and passed his flight test with flying colors. I issued him his instrument rating, and the very next day this 83-year-old gentleman took a Comanche to Florida (some 1,100 miles away) in hard IFR! I cannot describe the pleasure it gave me to issue the rating to that man.

Of course, when the paperwork hit the FAA, they questioned the 800 hours of instrument instruction that this charming old man had, but I had anticipated this and photocopied his logbook.

11

Although examiners are strictly forbidden to teach while administering a flight test—we are there to evaluate only—all examiners dispense a few tips, gems of knowledge acquired by years of experience in the airspace.

For example, most applicants, as part of the walk-around inspection during the preflight, will run the flaps down to the fully extended position in order to inspect the flip hinges, rollers, and attach bolts for safety and for excess play. If the airplane is a Cessna with 40 degrees of flap, the examiner may point out that if the pilot were at a distant airport and the flap motor burned out during the extension, the pilot would be stuck where he is until repair could be accomplished. However, if the flaps were to be extended only 10 degrees, the pilot could see anything he needs to inspect, and if he should be unable to retract the flaps, he could get in his airplane and go home.

Another such tip: Most instrument applicants, after they get their clearance, while still on the run-up pad, will set up their nav radios for the first en route fix. A knowledgeable pilot will set up his radios for the come-back—that is, for the approach in use at the departure airport. If, right after liftoff, you should punch into the clouds and, on your first scan of the engine gauges, observe the oil pressure needle bouncing on zero and the oil temperature out of sight, it would be no time to be looking up the approach to get back on the ground. There would remain perhaps five minutes until the engine seized. But if you punch into the clouds right after liftoff and all gauges are in the green, there's plenty of time to set up your first en route fix.

These are just two examples of the kind of teaching an examiner may do during the debriefing of the applicant.

In administering an instrument flight test, if he can, an examiner may arrange for the applicant to get a clearance to something other than an airport (a VOR, NDB, intersection or some such). If the applicant should accept such a clearance limit without demanding an expect further clearance time, it is time to counsel the applicant. Surely he was taught to NEVER accept a clearance to anything except an airport without getting an expect further clearance time. What does he do if he loses com—make donuts in the sky at the clearance limit until he runs out of fuel, then crash and burn? When ATC, in a sincere effort to help the pilot, issues such a clearance just to get the pilot started along his way, the controller almost invariably neglects to issue an expect further clearance time. And when the pilot asks for an expect further clearance time, he is usually told, "Oh, you can expect your filed route after such and such," the fix to which he was cleared. The pilot then asks, "What do I do if I lose com?" At this time the controller wakes up and issues an expect further clearance time. What this little exercise does is give the examiner an opportunity to emphasize what the applicant's instructor has taught.

12

In an effort to do a perfect job, pilot applicants almost invariably exceed the tolerance when they plan a cross-country flight on a check ride. And this is true for applicants for the private, commercial, or instrument (the three kinds of flight test requiring cross-country planning). The applicant is supposed to plan, within 30 minutes, a trip near the maximum range of the airplane, considering fuel (with reserve), loading, wind, and so on. Even though this is regulatory, I don't know of a single applicant in all my experience who succeeded in completing his planning in the allotted 30 minutes, nor do I know any other examiner who has had an applicant do so.

Unlike most tasks, this one allows the examiner quite a bit of leeway (he can allow extra time if the applicant is put on hold by flight service when he calls for a weather briefing, etc.), but when the 30 minutes stretches to much over an hour, most examiners find it a bit much. Personally, after about 45 minutes, I check with the applicant to see how he's doing and make some pointed remark such as, "One reason people fly airplanes is because they go fast, and if it takes more than 30 minutes to plan a three-hour flight, it's indicative of weak planning ability. Let's get going and wrap this up in the next five or 10 minutes!"

We all know that once the applicant is issued his certificate or rating, he will probably never again draw a line on a chart nor will he look at his computer until he has to take another examination (written or flight). However, in the test situation, the applicant is so anxious to get everything right that it seems to take forever. Once he has the certificate or rating, the situation changes: He gets in the airplane, takes off, points it in the general direction of his destination, and blunders around the sky for a while, and if he's lucky, after a while he arrives where he wanted to go. I remember reading an article several years ago about a flight instructor at Teterboro who walked out on the ramp and saw a former student of his standing by a Bonanza with sectional charts spread over the wing and down onto the ramp. The Bonanza pilot was drawing lines with a yardstick, and the instructor asked him what he was doing. The pilot replied that he was planning a trip to Florida, whereupon the instructor folded up all the charts, handed them to his former student and said, "Take off, go that way (pointing east), and turn right at the first ocean you come to. After a while you'll get to Florida."

That's a gross exaggeration, but its more like what a pilot is likely to do in the real world than what the examiner sees on a flight test. With all the wonderful navigation devices available today, true pilotage has almost become a lost art. Most VFR pilots navigate by VOR, loran, or GPS, even in perfectly clear weather. They don't draw a course line on the chart, mark off check points, and work up a long trip log. But they must be able to do all these things, and do them accurately on the flight test, to demonstrate their ability to do so to the examiner.

Most private applicants have a difficult time planning a trip that requires them to turn the sectional chart over and continue their course line on the other side of the chart, so naturally when I give the trip-planning assignment to an applicant, I have him plan a trip that requires both sides of the chart be used. This is a skill the applicant should have acquired in training, and I'm merely checking.

Does that make me mean? Perhaps I'm just less lenient than some. One pilot examiner (a former FAA inspector and accident-prevention specialist) said, "Pilots don't have accidents because they are deficient at cross-country planning." Oh? Then why do so many pilots run out of fuel?

13

Many instrument rating applicants I fly with are having trouble with partial-panel approaches, copying clearances, and flying DME arcs.

One of the required operations on the instrument flight test is a nonprecision approach flown with the use of partial panel only, that is, without the use of the attitude gyro and the heading indicator. A turn coordinator or rate-of-turn indicator is the only gyroscopic instrument used in partial-panel flying.

Most of today's pilots are taught to fly on the gauges with near-total dependence on the artificial horizon, and they become quite helpless when they lose it. Reliance on the attitude indicator is essential if you fly jets, but that's why jets have three attitude gyros and light airplanes only have one. Of course, when you lose the attitude gyro in a light airplane, you are also likely to lose the directional gyro, since both are usually powered by the vacuum pump, and the pump is the least reliable component of the system.

I find that applicants who fly best on partial panel are those who were taught to use the heading indicator (or gyroscopic compass) as the primary bank instrument and the altimeter for primary pitch information. These pilots use the attitude gyro as a "performance instrument," looking at it only when they want to make major changes in attitude. If you normally look to the altimeter for pitch information, you won't miss the attitude gyro too much when flying partial panel. And the turn coordinator is a reasonable replacement for the directional gyro as primary bank indicator.

Another area where instrument applicants frequently err is in correctly copying the clearance when we start out on the flight portion of the practical test. We usually file a round-robin flight plan, from Airport A to Airport A via Airport B with multiple approaches at B. A substantial portion of applicants become so fixated on the fact that they are going to B that when they read the clearance back, they say that their clearance limit is B, forgetting that they are actually cleared back to A. A typical instrument practical test clearance goes something like this: "ATC clears Swiftbird N1234 to Alpha via Homebase Departure 4, fly runway heading for vectors to X-Ray Intersection, direct Bravo, direct, climb and maintain 3,000, expect 6,000 10 minutes after departure, departure frequency is 132.2, squawk 5121." (Note that the second "direct" refers to the return to Alpha.) When the stressed-out applicant reads this back, he usually gets it all right except for the elimination of the second "direct." In other words, he has read back a clearance to Bravo only, and this is his mental clearance limit, although his actual clearance limit (in the system) is Alpha. The unfortunate thing is that the controller response is usually (but not always) "Readback correct!" In this case I have to correct them both. Of course, sometimes the controller corrects the applicant, but they don't always catch this error, and if anything, the mutual understanding of clearances must be exactly precise. Each party to the communication must know exactly what the other not only said, but what he meant. This is, after all, a test we're about to fly.

One of the most useful, but seldom-used, techniques in the repertoire of the instrument pilot is the DME arc procedure for maneuvering to intercept the final approach course. Most instrument instructors work in a radar environment virtually all of the time and they barely touch on DME arcs, if they cover it at all. But, as an examiner, I may ask you to demonstrate the use of any equipment in the airplane, and this includes the DME if the airplane is so equipped. In other words, if it's in the airplane (whatever "it" is), the applicant is expected to know how to use it. This also includes the autopilot, and since most instrument instructors require the trainee to fly the airplane manually throughout the training experience, we will occasionally find an instrument applicant who has an autopilot-equipped airplane and doesn't know how to use it—or at least doesn't know how to operate all its modes.

Dear Editor:

In October's "Eye of the Examiner," Howard Fried says, "We usually file a round-robin flight plan . . ." Who files the flight plan? If the instrument applicant files the flight plan, isn't that illegal? He/she doesn't have an instrument rating. If Mr. Fried files the flight plan, isn't he then the pilot-in-command? If the examiner is pilot-in-command, then how can the applicant be sole manipulator of the controls, log the ride, and pass the exam?

Mr. Fried's contention that the attitude gyro is not a primary instrument contradicts FAA recommended procedure and the technique used by reputable schools, qualified instructors, and designated examiners. Have I missed something else in my training?

Mr. Fried's comments about proficiency with all available equipment and DME arcs are well taken. Hitting one out of three will get most major leaguers into the Hall of Fame.

Sincerely,

P.P.

October 5, 1992

Dear Mr. P_____:

Thanks so much for putting me in the Hall of Fame with only a 333 average! The editors of *Flying* have forwarded a copy of your letter of September 24th to me and I feel compelled to answer it personally.

By regulation (FAR 61.47) unless he specifically agrees in advance to act as PIC, an examiner is not PIC when he administers a flight test. Thus, an individual who holds only a Student Pilot Certificate (and is prohibited from carrying passengers) is authorized to act (and log PIC time) while he is carrying a "passenger/observer" (the status of the examiner) on a check ride.

Under the same rule, an instrument applicant may act as PIC during the check ride!

Also, please be advised that the FAA currently holds that in a "stable flight condition" the attitude gyro is never primary for anything—it is a performance instrument and only comes into play when the pilot wants to do something. I refer you to the definition of "primary instrument."

Anyway, thanks again for the letter,

Sincerely,

Howard J. Fried

14

For many years I have been severely bothered by the fact that in pilot education (safety) meetings and in flight instructor clinics, the FAA talks down to pilots. They treat us as though we are all kindergarten children. Just like everyone else, I don't enjoy having my intelligence insulted with the simplistic presentations made at these meetings and in the manuals published by the FAA. And I certainly hope my column does not convey the same impression.

The mail response to this column has been phenomenal and mostly negative in nature. In spite of carefully researching my material, I have been accused of misstating facts, of being unfair to applicants, and, most unkind of all, of insulting the reader. The purpose of "Eye of the Examiner" is to educate, not to talk down to or insult pilots. Just as studying accident reports helps us avoid accidents, reading "Eye of the Examiner" should help CFIs to better prepare their applicants and thus reduce the number of busts on check rides.

Everybody takes check rides, and if the experiences, ideas, and suggestions contained in "Eye of the Examiner" serve to help an applicant at flight-test time, then I have served my purpose. Whether presented as a positive suggestion to help an applicant pass his next check ride or a negative factor to be avoided by future applicants, each column has had (and will continue to have) a message for the reader.

Here's an illustration of a fairly common error: On a private pilot check ride when the applicant does the simulated instrument work, after climbs, turns to a heading, descents, and unusual attitudes under the hood, I ask the applicant to tune a nearby VOR (there are several in the area) and fly right to it. A substantial number of applicants, having been taught that a radial is always "from," will center the needle with a "from" indication, then turn to that heading and start flying away from the station. Of course, if the pilot manages to keep the needle centered (by reverse sensing), we will ultimately get there, but it will be later rather than sooner since it is a 25,000-mile trip, during which several fuel stops would be required. And we'd get pretty cold going through the polar regions. Does this sound like sarcasm? Actually I'm hoping that this farfetched image will stick where the textbook learning clearly has not.

In a previous column, I mentioned the careless manner in which some applicants run through the check-off list. This business of believing that many, if not most, pilots are very perfunctory in their use of the checklist is by no means my idea alone. Here's an excellent example of this principle: A flight instructor tells me that the needle in the oil-pressure gauge in a trainer he uses would stick at the left end of the gauge when the engine was started and would remain there until the pilot tapped on the face of the instrument, at which time the needle would jump to the proper reading. Now, this instructor always teaches his students to physically touch each item (instrument, control, switch, breaker, etc.) on the checklist as they read it off. In the airplane with the sticky needle, four consecutive flight students were reading the check-off list, and coming to "oil pressure," all four put a finger on the instrument (and seemed to look right at it), while they said out loud, "Oil pressure coming up." This while staring at a gauge on which the needle hadn't moved off the peg. The instructor would then tap the face of the instrument and wake up the needle, explaining to the student that there is no use using a checklist unless each item is really checked. How's that for looking but not seeing, or seeing but not registering, or whatever? If telling this story makes one person use a checklist more carefully, it's served its purpose.

15

I have previously covered the subject of the nervous applicant with "checkitis," but there's another side of the coin. Once in a while I'll get to see an applicant who will attempt to intimidate the examiner.

This guy will start off with an air of extreme confidence as he lets the examiner know that he, the applicant, is indeed superpilot. Then it gets worse. He will voluntarily spout large quantities of erroneous "facts." He is "often wrong, but never in doubt." When he comes up with a wrong answer on the ground, he wants to argue with the examiner, and in the air if he blows a maneuver, he always has an excuse, or asserts he did it right, or "that's how my instructor taught me to do it." This know-it-all individual may very well pass his flight test, but he's likely to be a hazard to himself and others once he's turned loose in the airspace. We've all seen this guy, while he's still a student pilot, hang around the FBO and tell the ATPs how to fly.

Quite a different type is the high-powered business or professional person who is used to giving orders to subordinates (and having them instantly obeyed). He shows absolutely no respect for his young instructor, and when check-ride time comes, he attempts to intimidate the examiner.

It is predictable with absolute certainty that unless both of these two types change their attitude we'll be reading about them and their aviation adventures in the paper one day. Sooner or later they're bound to get themselves into serious trouble. The lesson here for the young instructor is to be very firm with the first type; and as regards the second type, to force himself to realize (emotionally as well as intellectually) that in the field of aviation, the instructor is the expert. No matter that the student pilot has far surpassed the instructor in age, wealth, and academic achievement (perhaps he's a doctor, attorney, or college professor), but in aviation he's the neophyte, and the flight instructor is the pro. Once the instructor establishes this, both in his own mind and in the mind of the student, training can take place; but until this happens, there can be no learning (or effective teaching).

It is, of course, the instructor who must set the tone of the relationship that exists between himself and the student, just as the examiner must control the relationship between himself and the applicant. This teacher-pupil relationship has to be established immediately at the first meeting, or there are those who will attempt to bully the instructor into permitting them to determine the course of their training. The flight instructor must bear in mind that, in general, he is responsible for whatever his students do, and no one likes to assume responsibility for that over which he has no control.

It is the rare applicant who tries to play mind games with his examiner, but it does happen. The bottom line is, be honest and forthright with your examiner, and don't try to bluff him or argue with him. This doesn't mean that if you have a valid point to make you should stifle it, but rather that you should politely interject your point. It will no doubt be given the consideration it deserves.

16

In a recent issue of a popular aviation magazine, there was an article stating that most, if not all, designated pilot examiners either can or think they can tell if an applicant will pass or fail a check ride in the first five minutes. Although I personally knew one such examiner who claimed to have that ability, I'm here to tell you that I certainly don't. I never know for sure what the outcome of a test will be until the last item is covered, the last task completed.

The author of the article stated that examiners have the ability to predict the outcome of a flight test almost immediately, based on the smoothness or lack thereof with which the applicant manipulates the controls of the aircraft. While it is certainly true that the smoothness of the pilot's actions are indicative of his skill as an airplane manipulator, passing a flight test requires a great deal more than this. The objective of each task as published in the Practical Test Standards for that particular certificate or rating must be met, and this involves infinitely more than merely being a smooth manipulator of the controls.

It is a real source of pleasure to me to observe one whose hand is so light on the controls that when a change in flight conditions is effected you wonder just when and how it was accomplished, but this alone does not get the job done on a check ride. In fact, an average (or slightly below average) airplane manipulator who has exceptional judgment will be a better *pilot* than the one who flies the airplane with flawless perfection but is lacking in good, sound judgment. Just ask yourself: Would you rather be a passenger in an airplane flown by a person who controls the airplane through the sky with flawless perfection but who lacks the good judgment to keep out of trouble, or sit behind one who is just an average flier but who has impeccable judgment and who uses his judgment to avoid trouble? The answer to that one is pretty obvious, isn't it?

As a flight instructor, the very best student I ever trained was just an average klutz as an airplane manipulator, but one who exhibited absolutely outstanding judgment. This student was a young woman, a medical doctor (head of a department at a large urban hospital) who had laid off for a month to have a baby, and then took an additional month to acquire a private pilot certificate. Twenty-eight days from the day she started training, she passed her private check ride, and the 28 days were the month of February, here in the northern Midwest, where we have an absolutely rotten climate. She got a 98 on her written and was upset because she missed a question.

Every weekday morning (she didn't fly on Saturday or Sunday) when I would arrive at the airport, I would find her standing on a ladder scraping ice and snow off the trainer she was using. We would fly a lesson first thing in the morning, and while I went about my other business, she would study. Over lunch we would continue her ground training, and then in the afternoon we'd have a second flight lesson every day. On the days the weather required us to stand down, she studied, and exactly 28 days from the start, this wonderful lady completed her primary flight training and passed her flight test (with another examiner).

She then really shot me down—she informed me that she had only done this to please her husband. I had already trained her husband for his instrument rating, and now, some 20-odd years later, the son whose birth gave his mother the maternity leave and the time to learn to fly is a flight instructor himself and an aeronautical engineering student at a great university.

The whole point is, I would rather have my children in the back seat of an airplane flown by this woman, who exercises impeccable judgment, than behind many very smooth pilots I know who take unnecessary chances and otherwise demonstrate poor judgment. And an applicant's judgment takes more than five minutes to assess.

17

The highest pinnacle to which an aviator might aspire is to be a truly great flight instructor, for certainly the primary flight instructor is the most important individual in the entire aviation community. Think about it—there isn't a high-time captain operating one of those flying condominiums across the big puddle, there isn't an astronaut who stepped on the moon, who didn't start with a primary flight instructor from whom he acquired the habits that have carried forth throughout his entire aviation career.

As I mentioned in a previous column, the FAA assumes the posture that the student can do no wrong. If an applicant is properly prepared, there is no excuse for him to bust a check ride, and it's up to the instructor to get 'em properly prepared! If, perchance, an applicant should fail a flight test, it means nothing significant to him (except a postponement of his certificate or rating and a few more dollars invested), but it goes on his instructor's permanent record. And the FAA tells me that if an instructor scribbles his signature on the 8710.1 (application form) so that it can't be deciphered, if the applicant passes, the instructor doesn't get credit for a passed applicant. But if the applicant fails, they look up the CFI's number and charge him with the bust! It is the instructor's record that is on the line, not the applicant's, and this is as it should be.

Proper pilot preparation all starts with the Practical Test Standards. It is absolutely unbelievable how many applicants (and not just private pilot types) show up for a flight test without ever having been exposed to the PTS, or indeed, totally unaware of the existence of such a thing.

The government does pilots a huge favor by laying out in excruciating detail exactly what is expected of an applicant. The PTS details every required procedure and maneuver, establishing the exact standard to which a pilot will be held in the performance of them; yet it is often ignored. I believe it is almost criminal for an instructor to send up an applicant for certification without having briefed him completely on the appropriate PTS.

It is the PTS, not time in your logbook, which should determine when you are ready to take a check ride. With the increasing sophistication of the equipment we operate and the environment (complex airspace) in which we do it, it is a constant source of amazement to me that anyone can acquire sufficient knowledge, experience, and skill to achieve the exalted status of Private Pilot in anywhere near the minimum number of flight hours required by the FAA. Not only is it a monumental task for the student to acquire the knowledge, experience, and skill to qualify for the certificate or rating for which he is applying, but it is an equally difficult job for the instructor to get him ready—an accomplishment that the instructor is certifying when he or she signs the recommendation on the back of the 8710.1.

18

One of the most important items an applicant for a commercial pilot certificate must know is the exact privileges and limitations of his certificate. To understand what a commercial pilot can and cannot do, you must understand the difference between FAR Part 91 rules, which govern personal and business flying, and Part 135 rules, which regulate charter and some scheduled airline operations. The commercial pilot applicant often shows up for his check ride with a gross misunderstanding of these rules. He either thinks that if he earns the commercial he can do anything at all in an airplane to earn money, or he is deluded into thinking that he can do hardly any kind of commercial flying.

I try to probe for an applicant's understanding of the difference between FAR 91 and FAR 135 flight during the oral quizzing by posing a couple of hypothetical situations. First I tell the applicant that he has just learned that his associate Bill is in the hospital in a distant city (auto accident or some such) and Bill wants his wife, Nancy, at his bedside. Bill would like the applicant to bring Nancy to him in the applicant's airplane (either owned or rented). Nancy will pay for his services and the cost of operating the airplane. May he do this? The answer is "no." That flight in which the commercial pilot is flying an airplane he owns or controls is governed by Part 135 charter rules. (Of course he could offer to do it for nothing, in which case it would be perfectly legal, but that's not the point.)

In the next scenario, Bill asks the commercial pilot to fly Nancy to his hospital bed in Bill's Bonanza; Nancy will pay for his pilot services. May he legally do this? Yes, because he is providing pilot services, not an airplane. The real point here is that, reduced to its simplest, the crucial difference between Part 91 and Part 135 boils down to who owns or controls the airplane. If one supplies both an airplane and pilot to another for compensation, it is a Part 135 flight. But if one provides only pilot service to another who owns or controls the aircraft, it falls under Part 91.

Many new commercial applicants don't realize that they can be employed and paid as a corporate pilot, for example, flying the executives of the company that owns (or controls through a lease agreement, or whatever) the airplane, the equipment of the company, and the guests of the company. But if the guests pay for the trip, it then falls under Part 135 rules and the company owner of the airplane would be required to hold a 135 air-carrier certificate and the pilot would have to be named on the operation specifications of the certificate. The primary exceptions to this are flight training, sightseeing flights that take off and land at the same airport, and flight to carry parachutists. In these circumstances the commercial pilot may provide services in an airplane he owns or controls without falling under Part 135 rules.

Because these distinctions are located in widely separated places in the regulations, it is up to the instructor to carefully explain the privileges and limitations of the commercial certificate to his trainee so that the applicant may be well prepared in this area. It is part of the instructor's function to ensure that his applicants are well prepared, and this includes knowledge as well as skill. It is in the area of "aeronautical knowledge" that some instructors are failing to do the job. They seem to think that their only function is to teach the student to manipulate the airplane (the "aeronautical skill" requirement) and that if the trainee did well on the written examination, the knowledge requirement is already taken care of.

The good instructor thoroughly covers all the tasks delineated in the Practical Test Standards prior to recommending the applicant for his certificate or rating and will give the student a simulated flight test before turning him over to the examiner. This is automatically accomplished with the graduation ride at schools operating under Part 141. A pilot trained to the less-structured rules of Part 61 should have the same degree of preparation.

19

Although the area of responsibility with which "Eye of the Examiner" deals is flight tests (certification check rides), this time we will address the preparation for written examinations. In other words, you will now get your Old Dad's handy-dandy method of beating the written exam. Of course we don't mean actually cheating, but rather an almost surefire way of passing with a good score.

To start with, you must acknowledge two things: First, there really are no trick questions—all the questions are straightforward, but if you miscalculate, you will likely find your (wrong) answer among the choices. And second, most people fail writtens not because they don't know the material, but because they aren't answering the questions as asked.

Now, how to go about passing once you get to the test location (and this system works whether you are taking the test at a computer test center or with a written test examiner): First, carefully look over all the materials (performance data for the hypothetical airplane you'll be dealing with, sample pages from the *Airport Facility Directory*, sample charts, and so forth). Read over the instructions very carefully. Then, being sure to answer the questions in the right slot on the answer sheet, go rapidly through the entire test, answering all the questions for which you know the answers without any doubt whatever and which need the least computation. Skip over any questions about which you have any doubt, which require any real thought, or which require any problem-solving.

Having done this, you've probably already passed the test with a score of 70 or better. Now go through the test again. Answer all questions that require problem-solving, being careful to make all necessary conversions (miles per hour to knots, true to magnetic, and so forth). Continue to skip those about which you have any doubt.

Now you're up in the mid-80s at least. And remember, although I don't believe it's true, the FAA says that 70 is as good as 100 on a written. Anyway, now try for that high-90s or 100 score. Go through the test again for a third time. This time we'll use logic to get rid of the obviously wrong answers. On those forms of the written that give the applicant four choices, there are usually two that are obviously wrong, and on the test forms that offer three answer choices, one is usually clearly wrong. Discard that one (or those two), and between the two remaining choices, toss a coin.

I know this system works, because for a period in excess of 10 years I taught a ground school with an enrollment of well over 50 students twice a year, and our pass rate on the written was nothing less than fantastic. Of the first 550 graduates from this private pilot course, we had three busts! And this was at a time when the national average pass rate was running in the 60th percentile. Does this system of taking FAA written tests work? You bet it does.

20

Today I lost an important source of business—a flight school that has been sending me approximately 20 applicants per year. The reason is that I busted a private applicant when, halfway through the check ride, I asked him to put on his hood or Foggles, and he didn't have either. As I explained in a previous column, my policy regarding the applicant who shows up for a flight test without a view-limiting device is: If I notice the lack of a hood or Foggles prior to takeoff, I offer to lend the applicant whichever he prefers. However, if we actually get in the air, and halfway through the flight test, without my having noticed, I refuse to go back and get the Foggles or hood. After all, it's not my responsibility.

The Practical Test Standards includes a checklist for taking the flight test, and it starts off listing "Item One, bring an airplane, Item Two, bring a view-limiting device!" My policy of disapproving the application of the person who shows up for his flight test without the required view-limiting device may seem cruel. It is certainly an expensive lesson for the applicant, but it is also certainly justified.

A few years ago a flight instructor absolutely came unglued when I sent an applicant back with a pink slip for this reason. It was the CFI's first bust after a long string of successful applicants, and he thought I was simply awful for busting the guy for forgetting his hood. I checked with several other examiners, and with a few FAA inspectors, all of whom agreed that I did the right thing.

In today's case, the recommending instructor had shown the applicant my previous column, and had admonished him several times, "Don't forget your hood!" He tells me that he agrees with me completely, and that he got into a real knock-down drag-out fight with the owner of the school, who thinks what I did was an absolutely terrible thing to do. The owner of the flight school insists that hereafter all their applicants should go to a different examiner. There is an examiner on our airport who brings a hood for the applicant's use to every check ride, and the school owner wants all their applicants to be tested by that examiner in the future, rather than by me.

Being a pilot examiner is a frightening responsibility. After almost 20 years and nearly 4,000 flight tests administered, I still live in abject terror of the day when I issue a pilot certificate or rating to an applicant and then read his name in the paper a day or a week later. If an individual can forget something as important as a view-limiting device on his check ride, what else might he forget after I turn him loose in the airspace? Suppose he forgets to check his fuel supply prior to launching off into the blue, or something equally important?

A bust is an expensive lesson, but if requiring the applicant to come back for the hood work and pay for a retest forces him to think prior to each future flight, it is well worth it.

April 13, 1993

Dear Editor:

Much like seeing the futility of swatting at annoying house flies and then getting fed up to the point of swatting at them anyway is where I find myself with Howard Fried. While over the months I (and I'm sure others) have found myself both annoyed and enlightened by Mr. Fried's comments, the May column leaves me swatting. Both Howard and the flight school he maligns should remove their heads from the up and locked position and grow up. Flight training should be cooperative process between the instructors and the designated examiners involved in certification. Mr. Fried's use of his column to primarily chastise the flight school in question is a great waste of space in *Flying*. And the flight school prohibiting applicants from using Howard is guilty of waste as well. And Howard, I don't think that you will read of many pilots running out of fuel as a consequence of forgetting a view-limiting device.

Sincerely,

R.M.
ATP, FE, CFII/MEI

April 23, 1993

Sir,

Howard Fried is an amazing individual, busting a private applicant for
forgetting a view-limiting device after Howard failed to notice it prior
to takeoff. How could they depart and forget such an important item?
I can see the NTSB results now— "Cause of crash: No View-Limiting
Device." Will Howard fail to notice something equally as important,
such as fuel, on the next check ride? Most examiners are more responsible and don't forget such important items before they take off.
Instructors should give Howard the pink slip. I would send my students to a more responsible examiner.

R.R.

Dear Editor:

Reading Mr. Fried's May "Eye of the Examiner" column brought back some sad memories. The aeronautical university I attended temporarily lost its self-examining authority. The result was a windfall to the three DEs on Prescott's Love Field. Many complaints were generated as the result of a few bone-headed examiners, not just from the applicants, but from high-ranking faculty and staff.

I was disappointed to read about Fried busting a private applicant for something as small as forgetting the hood. This action may indeed have been justified for an instrument or commercial applicant. For him to kick a private applicant in the face for something like this will only serve to betray any trust that might have formed between the applicant and the system.

As an instructor, I have always sought examiners who bolster the learning experience. I have no problems with disapproving anyone who clearly shows they're not ready. The fact that Mr. Fried charges a recheck fee says it all. Oh, I'm not saying that he doesn't believe in his convictions, it's just that self interest goes a lot farther in shaping those convictions than we'd like to admit.

I wouldn't lose too much sleep over what else a private pilot might forget on a future flight. They will make mistakes—we all do. They will not meet every applicable completion standard on every flight from now on. You DEs know good and well that you can't and don't check everything. The main responsibility for that lies with the instructors. The only way our students will survive the mistakes they make is to have an instructor who insists on good habit formation from day one. People with good habits tend to recognize the mistakes—before they snowball into something more serious.

It seems to me that it would certainly be a mistake to recommend any of my students to Mr. Fried. I've always had the best results from the ones who avoid the appearance of scandal. No recheck fee!

Sincerely,

M.F.S.

Dear Sirs,

I have been an avid reader of *Flying* since I was 15. Since I am working my way up to CFI status, Howard Fried's articles are particularly interesting.

But I must take exception to his May 93 article, about busting a private student for not having a hood for the check ride.

Would Fried bust a private applicant who forgot to bring a log book or his written test results? No! It would not get that far. The student would be ineligible for the check ride. The responsibility to make sure that the applicant is eligible belongs to both the student and examiner.

If the student screws up and forgets, its the examiner's right to say "Nope, not today." If the examiner screws up and doesn't catch it before takeoff, he should allow the student to land and get the hood!

Punishing the student with a bust for something that examiner should have caught on the ground is unfair, and it is passing the buck.

After all, if the examiner forgets something as important as a hood, what else will he forget to check? Perhaps its time for Fried to have an attitude check, sans hood.

Sincerely,

J.A.

May 3, 1993

Attn: Editor, Flying Mail

I feel I must comment on Howard Fried's May article "Eye of the Examiner." This guy is truly a pompous ass. To fail a private pilot applicant because he did not bring a view-limiting device is like giving a ticket for doing 4 miles over the limit, legal but asinine. It was over 20 years ago that I took my check ride. My attitude toward flight examiners would have been forever tainted if I failed for not bringing a hood. My ride was thorough and fair. I would expect nothing less today. A friend of mine recently took his check ride. The examiners fee for one hour of ground and two hours of air time was $250.00. That did not include the plane. For that kind of money I would have expected the examiner to come prepared and to buy lunch.

M.D.

April 14, 1993

Transmitted via FAX
Subject: "Eye of the Examiner" by Howard Fried—May '93

Dear Mr. McClellan:

I find Mr. Howard Fried's actions as an examiner to be outrageous! In the May '93 "Eye of the Examiner," Mr. Fried states that he issues "pink slips" to applicants who forget to bring "foggles" in the aircraft on private pilot flight tests.

As an examiner, Mr. Fried has been taught that all FAA Practical Tests must end in either: (1) the issuance of the Certificate or rating being sought, (2) the issuance of a Notice of Disqualification (Pink Slip), or (3) the issuance of a Notice of Discontinuance. Since the applicant in Mr. Fried's article did not exceed any of the standards shown in the Practical Test Standards, the applicant's test was certainly not a failure; and while it was not a passing test either, because the test was incomplete, the only correct action would be a discontinuance. The "Notice of Discontinuance" applies anytime a practical test cannot be completed for such reasons as weather, illness, or the failure of a piece of equipment that must be used on the test. When an applicant forgets the "foggles" it is no different than for the applicant to become ill during the test or for the ADF radio to fail on the instrument flight test. These tests are simply incomplete and must be continued at a later time.

Mr. Fried reasons in his article that if the applicant forgets the "foggles," then as a pilot, he may someday forget to put fuel in the airplane. In fact, there is no basis for such logic, and conclusions such as these are beyond Mr. Fried's area of expertise. Mr. Fried's opinions as a psychologist are not being requested; he has simply been hired by the applicant and requested to determine if the applicant's training is complete and that the applicant meets the objective standards that are shown in the FAA's Practical Test Standards publication.

It is the role of the FAA and the Administrator to "foster and promote" aviation. The examiner's role is a very important one: To fairly and objectively represent the Administrator during an applicant's final evaluation process. In my opinion, Mr. Fried's actions were contrary to his role and contrary to a sense of basic fairness to the applicant. Please let your readers know that Mr. Fried speaks for himself only, and not for the many other examiners who would disagree with Mr. Fried's actions.

Thank you.

Sincerely yours,

E. Allan Englehardt
FAA Designated Pilot Examiner
DuPage FSDO, West Chicago, IL
cc: Thomas Accardi, FAA

August 5, 1993

Dear Mr. Englehardt:

It was a distinct pleasure meeting and discussing the certification process with you at the *Flying* cottage at Oshkosh last week. Although we agree on a great many principles, neither of us has changed his opinion regarding handling the applicant who shows up for a check ride without a view-limiting device or doesn't even know that one is required.

To restate my position, let me say that it is my understanding that the interrupted ride or "Notice of Discontinuance" is reserved for those instances *beyond the applicant's control*, such as unforecast weather, unforeseen breakdown of some piece of required equipment (such as you pointed out—a suddenly inoperative ADF on an instrument test), or illness on the part of the examiner or applicant. The Disapproval Notice, on the other hand, applies to the unprepared applicant, whether it is inadequate performance of a required TASK in the PTS or some other form of unpreparedness.

Obviously, if an applicant shows up without his logbook or written result I do not disapprove his application. I have even loaned an applicant a chart on occasion, and, as I have pointed out, if the applicant asks or if I notice the absence of a view-limiting device, I offer to lend him one (his choice of hood or foggles), but once we get in the air *it's not my responsibility*. And you should know that my column in *Flying* generates a huge amount of mail (mostly negative, which I call my "hate mail file," and that particular column brought me well over a score of letters, about 60 percent negative and 40 percent supportive.

I just received my copy of *Examiner Update* and there was your letter on the front page (same letter you sent to *Flying* of which I already had a copy). I hope Ron Bragg sees fit to publish this, my answer, in the next issue.

As far as speaking for myself alone, I have polled some thirty DPEs, and two to one they share my attitude and policy regarding this issue. You may be in the majority of aviators, but I'm in the majority of examiners. I brought the subject up a few years ago at both a FSDO examiner meeting and a PEST seminar, and the FAA seems to agree with me on this matter. I recommend that you discuss this with the general aviation operations people at your FSDO and see what they say. I like to think I'm open-minded, and I'm certainly willing to change if it can be shown that I should.

Once again, it was a pleasure meeting you and your son and talking with you at Oshkosh '93.

Regards,

Howard J. Fried

To the Editor

I would like to comment about a recently published magazine article that was written by an FAA designated pilot examiner. The article, entitled "Eye of the Examiner," was published in the May '93 issue of a widely read aviation magazine. In the article the examiner states that he issues "pink slips" to applicants who forget to bring "foggles" in the aircraft on private pilot flight tests. In my opinion, such action by an examiner is OUTRAGEOUS!

As examiners we have all been taught that all FAA Practical Tests must end in either: (1) the issuance of a Certificate or rating being sought, (2) the issuance of a Notice of Disapproval (Pink Slip), or (3) the issuance of a Letter of Discontinuance. Since the applicant in the article did not exceed any of the standards shown in the Practical Test Standards, the applicant's test was certainly not a failure; and while it was not a passing test either, because the test was incomplete, the only correct action would be a discontinuance. A "Notice of Discontinuance" applies anytime a practical test can not be completed for such reasons as weather, illness, or failure of a piece of equipment that must be used on the test. When an applicant forgets the "foggles" it is no different than for the applicant to become ill during the test, or for the ADF radio to fail on the instrument flight test. These tests are simply incomplete and must be continued at a later time.

In the article the author reasoned that if the applicant forgets the "foggles," then as a pilot, he may someday forget to put fuel in the airplane. In fact, there is no such basis for such logic, and conclusions such as these are beyond the examiner's areas of expertise. The examiner's opinions as a psychologist are not being requested; the examiner has simply been hired by the applicant and requested to determine if the applicant meets the objective standards that are shown in the FAA's Practical Test Standards publication.

The role of the pilot examiner is extremely important. The examiner must fairly and objectively represent the Administrator during the applicant's final evaluation process. This role requires adherence to the objective standards as outlined in the Practical Test Standards.

If you will, please point out to the public that the author of the "Eye of the Examiner" speaks for himself only, and not for the many other examiners who disagree with his actions.

Thank you.

Sincerely yours,

E. Allan Englehardt
FAA Designated Pilot Examiner
DuPage FSDO, West Chicago, IL

August 10, 1993

Dear Howard,

Since I always read your "Eye of the Examiner" column first thing with each issue of *Flying* Magazine, to actually meet you was the highlight of Oshkosh '93. I was pleased to hear your comments and thoughts about being an examiner. It may interest you to know that I found myself to be in agreement with almost everything you had to say. You may recall, however, that the one area of disagreement we had concerned your policy regarding applicants who forget to bring a view-restricting device or "foggles" to the flight test.

Howard, I feel somewhat embarrassed to think that when you returned home, you probably saw the FAA's *Examiner Update* with a somewhat critical letter to the editor that I had written on this very subject. I am sure you realize that letter was not intended as anything personal, but was only my own disagreement with your policy on this subject.

While there is some disagreement among examiners about how the test is to be administered, I believe that any disagreement is really because of a lack of administrative direction. I am presently working with the FAA and trying to identify the more significant areas of disagreement. I am hopeful that these areas will be clarified, and surprisingly, I am finding the FAA to be receptive to examiner input.

During our conversation, I remember your comments about the way things once were, when the FAA simply issued a set of Flight Test Guides and two booklets, one booklet with white certificates, and the other with pink slips, and the general instructions; "Issue the white ones when they pass and the pink one if they fail." I'm glad that the FAA is now trying to better serve the public by a more objective evaluation process.

I really believe that the applicants I test are the FAA's customers; and as customers, they should be treated with the fairness and respect that is so due. The fairness and respect that an airplane captain receives during an ATP practical test in a B-747 should be the same as that provided to a private pilot applicant.

Howard, I hope to see you again, and I will look forward to reading your column.

Sincerely yours,

E. Allan Englehardt

August 12, 1993

Dear Allan: (I guess that's how you like to be addressed by your friends, and I hope I may consider myself one such.)

Our letters must have crossed in the mail. I got yours of the 10th today, and, indeed we are in agreement on just about everything except the one issue.

I talked with Ron Bragg, head of the PEST (Pilot Examiner Standardization Team in OKC) a couple of days ago, and he says, "Once the test starts, you must disapprove the application if the applicant doesn't have a view-limiting device." I think you and I have to consider him the final authority on the subject. He says he'll print that view on the cover of the next "Examiner Update."

As I informed you at Oshkosh, my little column, "Eye of the Examiner," in *Flying* generates more controversy (and more mail) than anything else in the magazine. Most of the mail is negative in nature, and I have a huge file of what I call my "hate mail." That particular column broke the record for mail, and it has been almost evenly divided between favorable and unfavorable. The letters are still coming. *Flying* forwards all the letters dealing with the "Eye" column to me. I got one today from an examiner in Orlando, FL, and he supports my position.

As I said last time, it was a distinct pleasure meeting you at Oshkosh, and you may rest assured that I have not taken your criticism personally.

Regards,

Howard

July 26, 1993

"Eye of the Examiner"—May

Dear Howard,

I have seen a few publications condemning you for issuing a pink slip for applicant "forgetting" view-limiting device. The latest being in July "Examiner Update" full front page—with no *editorial* comment.

I retired two years ago after 50 years in general aviation—+30,000 hours—25 years as pilot examiner with estimated 10,000 FAA flight exams given, 35 years was chief pilot at Showalter Flying Service in Orlando.

On more than one occasion I have issued a pink slip for not bringing a view-limiting device. If the applicant was "bright" and could arrange a map or maps in a "slat" type limitation, I also permitted that arrangement.

I never considered myself a "hanging judge," always having trouble meeting our *15% suggested* (off the record) quota of pink slips.

I believe the pink slip came under checklists, which is a *requirement*. It clearly stated in test guides that view-limiting device was required, as well as suitable aircraft.

I had always believed that the FAA was a *reasonable* agency concerned with promoting safe pilots, but as I approached retiring, I felt the FAA had become more of a *bureaucracy* like other government agencies—interested only in *paperwork*—anyway—I'm in your corner.

BMB

April 28, 1993

Dear Editor:

I think that Howard Fried fails the "reasonable man" test when he busts an applicant during a check ride solely because the applicant failed to bring an instrument hood. Sure forgetting your hood for a check ride is a serious mistake, but is it grounds for a bust? I would think that this forgetfulness should certainly be considered in the final decision for pass/fail, but in and of itself should not be a deciding factor.

I also find it difficult to believe that a man who has given as many check rides as Howard would miss something like an applicant climbing into the airplane without a hood. This makes me wonder what his agenda is when he lets the guy fly half the check ride before dropping the hammer on him. Wouldn't it be better to send him home and tell him to reschedule the check ride when he is better prepared?

Failing an applicant on a check ride affects both the record of the applicant and the instructor, and should be reserved for instances where the applicant is deemed unsafe and/or incompetent to aviate on his own. While forgetting your hood is bad headwork, I don't think it meets that criterion.

As far as believing that this bust will teach the applicant something about checklists or fuel management, change the way he looks at every flight from now on and maybe save his life one day... Get a clue Howard! There are more effective ways of teaching people.

Blue Skies,

D.H.

Attn: Flying Mail

Congratulations to the flight school owner who is insisting that his students not go to Howard Fried for check rides. After reading Mr. Fried's column for several years, it's clear to me that he doesn't understand his place in the system, which is to ensure that pilots can safely fly in the real world (where they don't need a hood). Unfortunately, Mr. Fried's world is defined by the Practical Test Standards. Good examiners use the standards to determine if a pilot can handle real-world situations, not to defeat them in a nitpicking contest. The most respected and effective check pilots are tough and thorough while being fair and reasonable; they fail pilots who might be unsafe; they don't fail pilots with checkitis who overlook administrative details. Aviation would benefit if more schools rejected examiners like Mr. Fried.

Sincerely,

Ross Bowie

April 29, 1993

Flying Mail

I can't stand it any longer. Who does Howard Fried think he is? I thought his "pointed" comments to the private applicant (April issue) were pompous and unprofessional. I can't believe that he is surprised a flight school dumped him (May issue) when he pink-slipped an applicant for forgetting his hood. I can recall being wound tight on the day of my first check ride. I had heard all the usual horror stories about the local examiner. When I actually met him and realized that he was considerate and professional, my exam day "yips" were overcome.

I don't believe that forgetting a hood on exam day is indicative of a forgetful and poor pilot; it's more a result of Mr. Fried's reputation as a tyrant.

JF

Dear Sir,

I have been receiving your magazine for about a year, and it has some very well-written articles. One column that turns me off to the whole magazine is when I read the "Eye of the Examiner," by His Majesty—Mr. Perfect, Howard Fried. He continues to show his smug attitude, that is "greater than thou," and I got mine, you get yours.

It is very sad that the FAA and their examiners display this type of attitude instead of trying to display a little kindness. Taking any test is nerve-wracking enough, much less doing it in an airplane. I am sure that Mr. "Perfect" Fried has never in his entire flying career ever forgotten one simple item such as a view-limiting device.

I personally give the flight school all the credit in the world for not using him. He is a perfect example of the Federal Monster that the FAA has built itself to be. As long as Mr. Fried is writing for your magazine, I will not be renewing it this year. What the general aviation community needs is cooperation and kindness between one another and our Federal counterparts, not the Mr. Tough Guy attitude displayed every month by Mr. Perfect Fried.

This is written in response to the May article, "Eye of the Examiner."

Respectfully Submitted,

D.J.

16 April 1993

Gentlemen:

I agree with the school owner who doesn't send any more students to Howard (May—"Eye of the Examiner"). The examiner should determine that the applicant's practical checklist is completed prior to the flight. Failure to do so indicates laxity on the part of the examiner. I'll bet Howard doesn't forget to ask for his fee—that's also on the applicant's checklist.

I try to see that the applicant brings a hood—no foggles please—because it's how he performs under the hood that is the important thing.

GCJ

When are you going to fire Fried? He has been controversial since he started.

He is typical of FAA examiners we have seen for years. We don't have to pay to read him.

They take pride in rejections. Don't try to help a guy. They don't know what the real world is all about. Thank God there are some good ones, but the turkeys never learn.

The rejection in May issue is classic. How proud he was to turn the guy down—doesn't *Fried* have a checklist? He could have turned him down before takeoff.

C.W.L.

21

The vast majority of certified flight instructors in the United States are conscientious, thorough teachers who prepare their students completely, omitting nothing from the training curriculum. There is, however, a small minority, enough to make a significant difference, who do a simply terrible job of preparing their applicants to meet the standard established by the FAA and published in the Practical Test Standards.

Some of these folks are marking time while teaching, using their CFI as a steppingstone in their own careers while accumulating the experience to make themselves attractive to the corporate or air-carrier employer. Some are part-timers who love to fly but can only afford to do so at someone else's expense. The latter is the guy who keeps the student from getting needed hands-on training by repeating the demonstration of each procedure and maneuver again and again. He flies the aircraft while the student watches; the student is merely a passenger.

The former is a result of a system that demands that the pilot have a certain amount of experience before the carrier or corporation will (or can) hire him. The only reasonable way for the young aviator seeking career advancement to gain this experience is to instruct. Now, there's nothing inherently wrong with this just so long as the instructor gives his students the very best he can offer while he is in his teaching stage, and most do. With the experiment of some air carriers trying the concept of *ab initio* training, we may see a change in this system. Meanwhile, the instructors who are in it just to gain experience at their students' expense wonder why they have such a high bust rate (which also doesn't look too good on their resumés).

Most part-time instructors are teaching because they love flying and have a burning desire to pass on the pleasures of aviation to anyone they can, but, as mentioned, there are some who are flying at their students' expense—in more ways than one: Not only is the student being charged money for the instructor's pleasure, but he's also being short-changed in this training. And it shows up at check-ride time.

The really good instructor is so concerned with the welfare of his students that he gives unstintingly of himself. While following a structured course of instruction, he tailors the training to the individual personalities of the students. He encourages the timid learner to be more decisive and instills caution in the overconfident. The result of this kind of training is clearly demonstrated on his flight test by the applicant, who is likely to give the pilot examiner a letter-perfect check ride.

From experience with an instructor's students, the examiner after a while can form a pretty good picture. There are students who can make even the best instructor look bad; but after looking at a half dozen or so of an instructor's product, I can pretty well tell what kind of job that guy's doing.

22

The single-engine seaplane rating (as an add-on to an existing pilot certificate) has traditionally been sort of a gift, but since the advent of the Practical Test Standards, that is no longer true. Now the applicant must earn the rating by meeting the standard—and a fairly tough standard it is.

Basically, for any add-on rating, an applicant need not perform any tasks already done in acquiring the initial certificate of the same grade. As a result, formerly all a seaplane add-on applicant had to do were a few water takeoffs and landings and demonstrate proficiency at docking, beaching, and sailing, as well as understand the differences involved in the three kinds of taxiing (idle, plow, and step) and when to use each. In addition to centers of balance and pressure, the applicant had to understand the concept of center of buoyancy and how it reacts to differing speeds during water-taxi maneuvers.

Although the PTS doesn't specifically say so, today's applicant is expected to know quite a bit more. He must learn the rules of right-of-way on the water, the U.S. Coast Guard safety recommendations, buoys and their meanings, and so on. If we are to retain the freedom to use the water—any sizable body of water—as an airport, we must know and practice water etiquette.

As long as the applicant satisfactorily explains and demonstrates the tasks set forth in the PTS, he will be awarded the rating (Single Engine Sea), but if it is done in a hull (such as the Republic Seabee or Lake Amphibian), it is an entirely different matter than doing it in a floatplane. The techniques of flying and the water work in the two are so different, separate ratings should probably be offered, such as soaring people get.

All of which brings up another discrepancy in the regs. A few years ago the FAA created the multiengine rating as a rating on the instructor certificate because it is a class rating. The seaplane rating is also a class rating, but if a flight instructor has a seaplane rating on his pilot certificate, he is automatically a seaplane instructor. Makes a lot of sense, doesn't it? Just another area in which the regulations are inconsistent.

There are, of course, two ways in which the Single Engine Sea test is conducted: one, the full test for the original issuance of a private or commercial certificate, and two, the addition of the class rating to an existing private or commercial, which requires only those tasks not previously demonstrated at the time of the original issuance of the appropriate grade certificate. In both cases all the tasks unique to seaplane operations must be demonstrated and explained. These include such things as glassy and rough water takeoffs and landings, knowing how to operate with respect to winds and currents, suitable water landing areas, and so on.

Unless one has access to an amphibian (amphibious floatplane or a hull-type amphib), the seaplane rating is of very little practical use. It is, however, real old-fashioned fun flying.

Sat Jul 24 1993 09:37 am
Page 1 of 1
DATE: July 23, 1993
TO: Mr. Howard Fried
FROM: K. C. M., P.E. Aeronautical Engineering
1843940CFII/ME
SUBJECT: Eye of the Examiner

In the following fax, take in consideration my level of inexperience in seaplane operations. I have an SES in a J-3S and a MES in a twin Seabee, both from Jack Brown Seaplane School.

In your article about seaplane certification, you mentioned that flying the two different types of seaplanes was an entirely different matter. This may just be a difference in opinion in the definition of an entirely different matter. There might be a small difference in docking, in that hull seaplanes without sponsons do have wingtip floats that have to be considered. And you can climb out on the floats to assist in docking that you can not do with a hull-type seaplane. There would be a difference in pump out on the water between the types. And a difference in height above the water at which you flare. None of these differences, in my opinion, would require special certification.

The only real difference that I can see is the use of the ailerons during maneuvering on the water. Where the float plane pilot would provide full aileron deflection as a preventative measure against capsizing forces, the hull-type pilot would have to work the controls as necessary to keep the wings level and keep the wingtip floats from digging in.

It also may be a case where I am able to see the differences and operate accordingly, where many people need to be shown the differences because it is not obvious to them. You, I am sure, have more experience dealing with the many different piloting abilities that are out there. Actually, when you consider the abilities of the average pilot, there may be a need to add certification requirements because of the abilities. I tend to look at things through my own viewpoints and abilities.

If there is a case where there is a major difference in the operation of the two types, maybe someone should write an article explaining the different types of operations.

Yours truly,

K.C.M.

August 6, 1993

TO: K.C.M.
FROM: Howard J. Fried, AB, BS, MA, JD, SFIA&I SME, FIG, AIGI, ATP
ASMEL, CA, SES, CG
SUBJECT: Your fax of July 23rd

The editors of *Flying* have forwarded your fax to me and I feel compelled to answer it personally.

You are indeed correct in all your statements. However, it seems that your only experience in a hull-type amphibian has been in the twin Bee, and my reference was to the single-engine hulls (such as the Seabee and the Lake). There is a great difference in the handling characteristics of these as opposed to the float plane. This is primarily based on the fact that the engine is mounted on a pylon above and behind the cockpit and uses a pusher-type prop.

In this configuration, when power is applied, the nose pitches down, and when power is retarded, there is a very pronounced pitch up. This is, of course, contrary to the airplane, which has the engine(s) out front. This means that if a go-around should be required just prior to the flare, the pilot had better be prepared to really yank back on the yoke, or he's likely to find his nose in the ground (or water, as the case may be). There are also other differences resulting from having all that weight way up above, but that's the biggie.

I hope this clarifies my position for you.

Regards,

Howard J. Fried

23

There is one task in the Practical Test Standards for the Private Pilot-Airplane (Multiengine Land) class rating that is rarely properly taught to multiengine applicants. It was formerly called "the effects of airplane configuration on engine-out performance," but it is now listed as Pilot Operation 10, Area of Operation XII, Task D, "Demonstrating the effects of various airspeeds and configurations during engine-inoperative performance."

As an examiner, when I ask an applicant to demonstrate just how aircraft configuration affects performance with one engine inoperative, I usually get a blank stare, and a comment to the effect of, "What do you mean? Just what do you want me to do?" This, after I have carefully briefed the applicant on the fact that it's nothing about what I want, but rather what the PTS requires.

"Just show me how you were taught to do it," I say. "What I'm really doing is evaluating the quality of your training." I then get the old, "My instructor never showed me that."

At this time, I hand the applicant the PTS and let him read the definition of the task. The purpose of this exercise is to graphically bring home the degree of degradation of performance with a windmilling prop as opposed to a feathered one, of having the gear extended as opposed to retracted, of having flaps extended as opposed to retracted, as well as other changes (carburetor heat, for example, if we're working with a carbureted engine).

If the pilot latches on to VYSE (the published single-engine best rate of climb for a twin, with one engine inop), and holds that speed for several seconds (or a minute or two), when the VSI stabilizes he can note the reading. (It may not be climbing at all, but whatever performance there is will be found at precisely that speed, even if it is a least sink rate.) If we do this with the prop windmilling, and again with it set at zero thrust (simulating feathered), we can see just how important it is to feather the prop.

By comparing the climb, or lack thereof, with landing gear extended and retracted, with flaps extended and retracted, with both gear and flaps extended (by now, we're sinking like a rock!), we get a graphic demonstration of the importance of cleaning up the airplane when we lose an engine, as well as the priorities involved. Which is of more immediate importance, getting the flaps up or the landing gear? Very few flight instructors are very thorough in teaching this exercise.

Another multiengine exercise that is rarely taught, but which ought to be (even though it's not in the PTS) is a simple demonstration of the "critical engine" concept. Of course, this won't work if you are using a twin with counterrotating props, but with a conventional twin, if the VMC demonstration is held until the airplane starts to yaw away toward the dead engine with the left engine shut down, and then again with everything else exactly constant but with the right engine dead, the applicant will get a firm impression of just how much difference the critical engine makes. (In a 310 or a Baron it is at least six knots.)

Remember, VMC is a variable, and the published VMC is calculated under the worst possible conditions. Any change in these stated conditions is an improvement, and VMC will occur at lower than the published airspeed. Remember also that although the manufacturer of a light twin is required to publish a VYSE, nothing in the regs says that it must yield a positive rate of climb—under all conditions of altitude, weight, and temperature—it may very well only offer a least sink rate.

Dear Sir:

Howard Fried, I got ya! In your discussion of Vmc last month, you state, "...Vmc is calculated under the worst possible conditions. Any change in these stated conditions is an improvement, and Vmc will occur at lower than the published airspeed." This is simply not true.

    There are seven factors involved in determining Vmc, and three of the seven are "not worst" conditions. They are: standard day/sea level, maximum gross weight, and 3 to 5 degrees of bank into the good engine.

    I would be glad to explain how this is true, but that would require an entire article. Give me a call Howard, I'll give you some dual.

Sincerely,

S.F.

09-13-93

To JMM from HJF

If you opt to publish the letter from S.F. in "Flying Mail," here's my answer:

You're right, S_____. I said "worst possible conditions" for the sake of simplicity in training a multiengine pilot. It is certainly true that if one were in Death Valley (below sea level) on a cold day, it would be worse. Just as "takeoff flaps" are an improvement, so is the 3-to-5-degree bank a pilot is permitted to use in the demonstration. The operative word here is "permitted." The argument regarding gross weight has raged for years, and there is merit on both sides. On the one hand, at gross weight, a somewhat higher angle of attack must be used, and on the other, you have a greater mass going forward and thus a more pronounced force is required to get the yaw started.

Regards,

Howard

24

This time let's consider glider check rides. As is the case with any certificate or rating, the requirements for a glider flight test are set forth in the Practical Test Standards, of which there are two: one for the Private Glider and one for the Commercial Glider. The glider rating on a pilot certificate, whether it is an original or an add-on, involves a series of elements common to all sailplanes but will be restricted to one of three types of launch.

If the applicant is trained and tested only by means of the aero tow technique of launching the glider, his certificate will have a notation stating "Aero Tow Only." Conversely, if he is examined by way of winch or auto launch, his certificate will bear the restriction "Ground Launch Only." Finally, the applicant who demonstrates proficiency in a powered glider will have his certificate limited to that kind of glider operation only. Of course, each of these limitations may be removed by further testing. In other words, if a glider pilot whose certificate bears the notation "Aero Tow Only" demonstrates knowledge and skill in flying off a winch, the restriction is removed, and he receives an unrestricted glider certificate.

Although it is certainly unlikely that a demonstration of each would be feasible, or even possible, on the flight test, the applicant must be able to explain wave and ridge soaring as well as thermaling. Every glider student is taught to gain altitude by thermaling, but many have never had the opportunity to fly a ridge (flatlanders don't have ridges available unless they travel some distance), and very few have experienced the thrill of the wave. Even so, on the check ride they must be able to explain the safety factors involved in each as well as the techniques of soaring along a ridge and in a wave.

The glider pilot must also know and understand what kind of weather is best for soaring, how thermals develop, and where they may be found. Over what types of terrain is one likely to find lift? Stable or unstable air? Early in the day or late afternoon? Stratus or cumuliform clouds? Then there's the whole sphere of knowledge regarding signals, to and from the tow pilot or winch operator. All this is in addition to knowing the performance data of the machine being flown, when to use the best lift-overdrag ratio, when to speed up, and other information.

If the test is done with an aero tow, the applicant must box the wake of the tow plane and must demonstrate his knowledge and skill at removing slack from the tow line while attempting to maintain a proper tow position behind the tug. (Most glider training in the United States is done using the aero tow method of launching.)

Flying a glider is not particularly difficult, but it certainly is challenging. And the rewards are truly enormous. Personally, I can take my ATP certificate in my pocket, get in the pressurized, turbo-powered airplane and operate in the high-altitude structure, and that's enjoyable, but if I want to have real fun, I fly a glider. There's a thrill in gaining several thousand feet of altitude without an engine that just can't be matched.

25

If the examiner and applicant both agree, an "interested party" may sit in on the oral portion of any flight test. Indeed, the "interested party" may, if invited by both parties, observe the entire check ride, both ground and flight. I certainly consider the recommending instructor to be an "interested party." Therefore, ever since I became an examiner (almost 20 years ago), I have permitted the recommending instructor to sit in on the oral, and if there are enough seats in the airplane, to go along on the ride whenever I administer a certification or rating flight test.

My policy is as follows: From my viewpoint any flight instructor who is interested in the welfare of his student enough to take the time is welcome to attend, but the applicant has to invite him. After all, the applicant is the guy who is paying the freight. It is his money that's paying for the check ride. And the instructor's presence might very well add to the pressure under which the applicant is already laboring in the flight-test situation.

One of the major downsides to having the instructor sit in on the examination comes about as a result of the fact that applicants lie to the examiner. When asked a question about which they are unsure, the examiner invariably gets the classic "My instructor never taught me that!"—an excuse you can't very well use if your instructor is sitting right there. Even so, if the applicant can stand the extra pressure, it is a very valid experience for the instructor to go along and see exactly how the examiner handles the check ride.

It also helps, of course, to have that extra pair of eyeballs looking around for traffic while the examiner is devoting his attention to the applicant's performance. I'll never forget an incident that happened several years ago when I was giving a multiengine flight test in a tired old Apache. The applicant happened to be a flight instructor, and his instructor came along to observe his check ride for multiengine land privileges on his commercial pilot certificate. The applicant occupied the left front seat. I was in the right, and the observing flight instructor was behind me in the rear.

When I called for a maneuver that engendered a potential substantial loss of altitude (an imminent stall), the applicant—and remember, he was a flight instructor himself—yanked back on the yoke and stood the airplane on its tail without ever looking left or right or making any attempt whatever to clear the area around us. As the applicant did this I was looking out to the right, and I glanced back at the instructor, who was frantically looking around out the left window. I don't believe I've ever seen a more horrified expression than that which was on the startled face of that instructor.

Of course, the ride was terminated at that time, and the applicant was sent home with his pink disapproval notice. Neither his flight instructor nor I could bring ourselves to believe what we had seen. A flight instructor who failed to clear the area prior to potential altitude-losing maneuvers! I wondered just how effective an instructor that applicant could be if he did that. Was he a "do as I say, not as I do" kind of guy? Or didn't he teach his students any better?

That particular applicant certainly learned a lesson that day, a lesson which he will never forget. There isn't a pilot I know who would even think of turning his car into an intersection without carefully looking around, but some of these same pilots blindly make turns without doing so—and of all people, a flight instructor ought to know better. Since his own check ride that day, the applicant (who qualified for his multiengine rating on reexamination) has sent me numerous applicants of his own, and I found them to be universally well prepared.

26

From time to time when the FAA finds an area that is brushed over or ignored throughout the training environment, it instigates a campaign to emphasize that specific phase of flight training. Such is the case with knowledge of medical facts for pilots. In the last few years, the FAA has been placing emphasis on aeromedical factors and has been expecting pilot examiners to thoroughly cover this area on flight tests, at least by means of oral questioning. In the Practical Test Standards for private pilot, it is listed as Operation 1, Area of Operation I, Task F.

The applicant must know and explain the causes, symptoms, and counteractive measures for such ailments as motion sickness, hypoxia, hyperventilation, carbon monoxide poisoning, and sinus and ear problems, including spatial disorientation. He must also know and explain the effects of alcohol and drugs (prescription, nonprescription, and illegal) and how flight safety is affected by their use. With the popularity of scuba diving today, the applicant must also know the effects of nitrogen excess from scuba diving as it relates to crew and passenger in flight.

Another area that has recently come to be emphasized by the FAA is that of stall and spins. Ever since spin training was deleted from the primary curriculum and spin entries and recoveries were eliminated from the private pilot flight test, way back in 1957, there has been a raging controversy as to whether or not spin training should be required of all pilots. At this time, actual spin training in the aircraft is only required of airplane and glider flight instructors. However, this does not mean that handling spins is not a part of the knowledge requirement for the private pilot certificate; it is. And the examiner is required to test the applicant on his knowledge in this area, even though it may only be by means of oral quizzing.

Although airplanes vary greatly in the techniques required for spin entry and recovery because of differences in their design, there are certain elements common to any spin and certain standard techniques by means of which recovery may be accomplished. Today's applicant is required to know and explain these elements and techniques.

Flight schools and flight instructors have been teaching student pilots how to make a stall and recover, when what they should be doing is teaching stall recognition. If the pilot recognizes the impending stall before it happens, then he can prevent the stall, and without a stall there can be no spin.

Consequently, the Federal Aviation Administration is now placing emphasis on the requirement that all private applicants demonstrate basic knowledge of the mechanics of the stall, including a thorough understanding of the concept of angle of attack and all the factors that influence it.

27

One reason people fly is because airplanes go fast, and although thorough planning is necessary, there is no valid reason why a competent pilot shouldn't be able to plan a cross-country flight in a reasonable time. By regulation, an applicant is required to plan a trip near the range of the airplane, considering existing conditions of loading (fuel with reserve), weather, etc., within 30 minutes. And a good, well-prepared student should be able to do so. The PTS says that the applicant should complete a navigation log with check points, frequencies, etc., and he should identify airspace, obstructions, etc., as well as alternates along the way. And he should file a VFR flight plan. He may file it with the examiner rather than ATC (through FSS).

I am always amazed when I see an applicant who has never had the experience of being on a VFR flight plan. Here's a person who has had a minimum of three hours of dual and 10 hours of solo cross-country flying without ever being on a flight plan and taking advantage of the free insurance offered by our government! Can you believe it? It actually happens with about one in 20 of the applicants I see. In these cases we actually file while on the check ride. I'm surprised that the FAA has not made filing, opening, and closing a VFR flight plan (under the supervision of an instructor) a requirement for all student pilots; it should be.

It is in this cross-country planning stage of the test that the examiner can check the applicant's knowledge of the airspace regulations. And if the applicant plans the entire trip by pilotage and/or dead reckoning, you may be sure the examiner will require him to demonstrate his ability and skill at radio navigation. Conversely, if the trip is to be made entirely by use of VORs, the applicant can expect a radio failure.

One of the Tasks (the objective of which must be met) in the cross-country operation of the Private Pilot Practical Test Standards is the diversion to an alternate, and you can't get from "here" to "there" if you don't know just where "here" is. It is surprising just how many applicants do not know their exact position while flying cross-country. When a diversion to an alternate is called for, the applicant has to blunder around, figure out where he is, and then determine just how to get to the nearest airport and how long it will take to do so.

While the FAA insists that inspectors and examiners apply the principle of "no second chance," I'm sure that I'm not by any means alone in applying the policy of grading an applicant up for making a self-correction. If an applicant catches a mistake before I call it to his attention, and he promptly, effectively, corrects it, I let it go.

An example would be in the situation where the applicant starts to wander off course on the cross-country, discovers his error, and makes the appropriate correction before he gets 5 or more miles off. Also, on an instrument check ride, if an applicant sees that an approach isn't working out and initiates a call for a "missed approach," I have no problem with letting him have another shot at it.

Both the above cases demonstrate the applicant's good judgment and are the kinds of activity that deserve credit, even extra credit. In neither of these cases do I consider it giving the applicant a "second chance." He has merely recognized a problem and taken appropriate action, and I would hope that in the "real world" he would do exactly the same thing.

Although it is extremely difficult to evaluate judgment, this kind of self-correcting activity gives the examiner a clue as to how the pilot will react when confronted with other than a normal situation once he has been certified and turned loose in the airspace with the rest of us.

28

I can't for the life of me see how a student pilot can acquire the knowledge and skill required to earn a private pilot certificate in anything near the minimum number of training hours specified by the FAA. Back when the Piper J-3 Cub and Aeronca 7AC Champ were the primary training airplanes, the tasks of both the instructor and the student were much simpler, and students needed fewer hours to prepare for the check ride.

In the old days, the instructor concentrated on teaching the student to make smooth, coordinated turns by balancing the movements of foot and hand, and the student learned to manipulate the airplane through the sky. Instrument training in the private pilot curriculum consisted of the instructor pointing toward the sky and saying, "See that cloud over there? If you go in that cloud you're gonna die!"

The written examination consisted of a few questions on aerodynamics (lift, weight, thrust, drag, etc.), a few rules of the road (light signals, hemispheric rule, etc.), and a smattering of navigation and meteorology. And the written was offered in sections—theory of flight, weather, CARs (Civil Air Regulations—what are now FARs), etc. What we now know as VFR was called CFR—"Contact" flying based on the fact that one had visual contact with Mother Earth.

The private flight test consisted of a few maneuvers, stalls, spins, and landings. There was no cross-country planning or flying on the check ride. In the mid-1950s, the FAA made both the written and flight tests a great deal more practical by basing both on a hypothetical cross-country trip. This is, of course, a much more realistic and practical way of doing it. In those days private flying was not the efficient means of transportation that it is today, and most private flying was probably for recreational purposes only. Forty hours of training and practice was usually enough to prepare an individual for certification as a private pilot. And the instructor rating was just that—a rating on the pilot certificate, good indefinitely, not a separate certificate, renewable every two years as it is today. The sweeping changes in the certification process and instructor certification came in 1957. Over the years, spins were deleted from the private and commercial curriculum, and basic instrument training was added (enough to teach the applicant to keep the airplane upright while he gets out of IMC).

Today, the private applicant has a veritable mountain of material to master before certification. Flying the airplane was once the hard part; now it has become the easiest part of flight training. Because of the increased and increasing sophistication of both the equipment we use and the airspace we fly in, the knowledge required of a private pilot is actually greater than that required by the old ATR (that's Airline Transport Rating, not the ATP certificate it is today).

Nowadays, instead of looking out the window and navigating by pilotage, or using the magnetic compass and clock while dead reckoning along the way, we tune the vortac, or crank up the loran C or GPS, and go where it tells us. We refer to the "attitude indicator," which used to be an "artificial horizon" before it became an "attitude gyro," and to a "heading indicator," which used to be a "gyroscopic compass" before it became a "directional gyro." I do so wish they'd quit changing the terminology on us. I have a great sympathy for the poor student pilot today who has to learn all this confusing stuff.

29

Although there can be a vast difference in the interpretation of the FARs among the FAA regions and districts, when it comes to the administration of certification oral and flight tests, we all use the same Practical Test Standards. This means that whether an examination is given by an FAA inspector or a designated pilot examiner, whether it occurs in New York or in California, the applicant is held to exactly the same standard.

There is a widely held belief in the general aviation community that an FAA-administered check ride is more difficult than one conducted by an examiner, but there is no valid reason why this should be so. If the applicant is well prepared, he or she will pass just as readily in either case. As I've pointed out previously, I've been taking check rides all my life to add ratings and to maintain my currency as an examiner, and most of them have been with the FAA. I've busted two, and in both cases I knew just what I did wrong and when. As a flight instructor, I've sent a great many applicants to the FAA to be examined, and any who have failed would no doubt have also failed with an examiner. The fear among pilots and flight instructors of exposing themselves to the FAA for examination is groundless.

Certain kinds of flight tests can only be given by the FAA, specifically medical flight tests. An applicant who requires a certificate of demonstrated ability (waiver) must be tested by the FAA. For this kind of check ride, there is a specific procedure that must be followed. For whatever reason the applicant cannot meet the medical standard for his particular grade of pilot certificate, he must request that a letter be forwarded from the Airman Certification Branch in Oklahoma City (or perhaps the Civil Air Medical Institute) to his local district office (FSDO or GADO) requesting a special medical flight test and setting forth the procedures for that specific check ride. Then, when his training is completed and his instructor recommends him for certification, he goes to the district office for his flight test.

The test itself is specifically designed to ensure that he can safely operate an aircraft despite whatever handicap prevented him from obtaining an unrestricted medical of the appropriate class. Probably the most frequent type of waiver is issued for colorblindness. The test typically involves looking at signal lights from the tower to determine if the individual can identify the colors aviation red, white, and green.

Once a pilot has a certificate of demonstrated ability, he may add ratings (instrument, category, class) to his pilot certificate without an additional demonstration, but if he seeks a different grade certificate, he must again demonstrate his ability to hold the new class of medical certificate appropriate to that particular grade of pilot certificate.

Other than those who came to the FAA directly from a military background, many, but not all FAA inspectors were designated pilot examiners prior to becoming government employees. And when they retire from the FAA, again many (but not all) ex-inspectors become designees. After all, who is better qualified to be an examiner than one who has been doing it right along as an inspector? And, as pointed out earlier, we all use the same Practical Test Standards as our bible. This is the definitive word on the subject of flight testing. So it's really the same type of examiner working for the FAA or working independently as the FAA's designated representative.

One distinct advantage of taking a check ride with the feds is that it's free. The examiner's manual says, "You may charge a reasonable fee for your services," but the inspector is a full-time paid employee of the government, so no fee is charged. It's all part of the service paid for with our tax dollars, and over the years examiner fees have grown to the point that it has become a factor to consider when preparing for an examination. Call your local FSDO or GADO to make an appointment for an examination. FAA inspectors may not have the same schedule flexibility as a designated examiner, but you will be put on the schedule for a no-fee check ride.

The point is that it makes no difference where an applicant takes his check ride, or with whom. What really matters is the degree of preparation. If the applicant meets the standard, he'll pass, if not, he won't. It's just that simple, and all the rumors about the FAA bogeyman notwithstanding, it just doesn't matter where or with whom a well-prepared applicant gets his practical test.

It also makes no difference where or with whom he takes the test if he's not well prepared. He'll bust his check ride wherever he takes it and whoever administers it.

30

Many years ago when I was struggling to become a pilot, there was a saying that given enough patience, anyone could learn to fly. That may be true, but there are some people—even if they are capable of eventually passing their flight test—who just don't belong in the airspace. Unfortunately, unless they can't pass their medical exam, I know of no way to keep them out.

Let me tell you a true story about one of those people (I'll call him George). Honest—I'm not making this up.

I first heard from George when he called to arrange to train for his instrument rating. He told me he was in his fifties, had a Commercial Pilot Certificate (ASEL) issued years earlier on the basis of his military experience, hadn't flown for many years, and had been a military pilot during the Second World War (in fact he was an ace—five confirmed kills in the Pacific flying a P-51—and had the records to prove it). I enrolled him and assigned him to an exceptionally good flight instructor.

George said he expected he would require only a few hours of "brush-up." (Certainly his records indicated he'd already exceeded the experience requirement.) But after 30 hours of ground and 20-odd hours of flight training, he was still standing with his feet firmly planted on square one. When George would show up, the CFI would briefly review what they had done during the previous lesson before starting the new one. George acted as if he'd never heard of it. The man wasn't dumb—he was a successful stockbroker—but he could not retain anything for as long as 24 hours. After another 30 hours or so, we recommended that George give up flying and take up tennis or golf or some other activity.

He didn't heed our advice; instead, he went to another flight school and enrolled there. After another 30 or so hours of training, it took him four tries to pass, but the examiner from the flight school finally issued him his instrument rating. On his first pink slip (Disapproval Notice) there were five or six unsatisfactory items. On each subsequent attempt he would satisfactorily perform one or two of the items until finally all of the requirements were met.

I next heard of George about a year and a half later, when the manager of still another flight school called to schedule him for a flight test for his multiengine rating. Since I was the only qualified Cessna 310 examiner in the area, I reluctantly agreed to administer the flight test. Good old George showed up at the appointed time, and after 35 minutes of desperately attempting to drag a single correct answer out of him, I sent him back with a pink slip. I made a list: After 21 grossly inaccurate responses on questions ranging from weight and balance to VMC, I gave up and busted him on the oral.

The following week, he flew about 60 miles away to another examiner, who passed him and issued him a multiengine rating. A week later George died in an airplane crash during an attempted takeoff in instrument conditions.

The only way I know of that this tragedy could have been prevented would have been if someone along the line had been able to convince George he should not be flying. Although it's true that almost everyone can learn to fly, there are some people who shouldn't. But there really is no way of stopping someone who is determined—despite contraindications—to become a pilot. If your instructor suggests you take up golf or tennis and give up flying, seriously consider the advice. George was a perfectly nice guy, he just didn't belong in the airspace.

31

Recently a member of the Pilot Examiner Standardization Team of the FAA said, "There's no such thing as a marginal applicant." What he meant is that there are no gradations on a flight test; the applicant either meets the standard or he doesn't, no middle ground. This is because flight-testing is what is called "criterion-referenced" testing. Whereas the written tests have a cutoff score of 70 percent, the practical tests are an either-or proposition. The cutoff score here is, in effect, 100 percent. The applicant meets the standard or doesn't.

Even so, we all know that some applicants perform better than others, so that of two passing applicants, one "scores" better on the check ride than the other. The outstanding applicant far exceeds the minimum standard of the PTS, while the not-so-good applicant barely comes up to that minimum. Thus the latter is what most of us call a marginal applicant, performing at the very edge of the tolerances. At least in this regard, there definitely is such a thing as a marginal applicant, in spite of what the FAA says to the contrary.

The knowledge requirement for a rating or certificate is judged empirically by a passing score on the written examination and by criterion testing on the oral portion of the practical test. The experience requirement is met by the applicant's presentation of a logbook with appropriate entries attesting to his training and experience.

Virtually every flight school, and all flight instructors, train their students to exceed the minimum standards of the PTS. Many years ago I learned a basic principle of flight instruction. It goes like this: If you give your students any leeway, any tolerance, they'll exceed it; if you demand perfection, you'll get it. And it works. If an instructor calls for 3,500 feet give or take a hundred, the student will be any-where between 3,000 and 4,000. And he'll think it's all right! On the other hand, if you say, "Didn't I say 3,500? What are you doing at 3,510? (or 3,480?)," pretty soon you'll see him nail 3,500 right on the money. Then, when he goes for his check ride, it'll be easy, because here he will have tolerances—space to waste! The same principle ap-plies to the written exam. The final quiz we gave to our ground school graduates was much tougher than the FAA written, so an ap-plicant who passed our final and went to the FAA test with a gradua-tion certificate from our approved course was an absolute cinch to pass the FAA test. I'm sure this principle of training to a much-higher-than-minimum standard is very widespread and is practiced by most instructors and flight schools.

On the written exam an applicant can miss all questions in an en-tire area of knowledge, and so long as it doesn't comprise 30 percent of the total, the applicant can pass the test. However, on the flight test if one Task is unsatisfactory in a single Area of Operation, then that Pilot Operation is unsat, and the applicant fails the entire test. True, on the recheck he may be asked to only repeat the single Task en-tered on his Notice of Disapproval, but even so, he has failed the en-tire practical.

Examiners are instructed in no uncertain terms, "No second chances! Do not give an applicant a second shot at demonstrating a procedure or maneuver. If he doesn't get it the first time, it's all over!" But just when does the recognition and correction of a maneuver by the applicant become a "second chance"? If the applicant makes a timely self-correction prior to the completion of a maneuver, should he not get credit for that? I think so, don't you?

01/21/94

Flying Magazine

"Eye of the Examiner" (Feb 94) claims that most flight schools train students to exceed minimum standards and recommends that an instructor criticize a student when altitude varies 10 feet from the assigned altitude.

This is a lot of baloney, and not the way students are treated during flight training. Current and prospective students should not be discouraged from flight training if they conclude from these statements that flight instructors have unreasonable expectations.

Flight training begins with reasonable expectations (as an example, maintain assigned altitude plus or minus 100 feet). When the student can perform all required tasks within the standards (it is not possible to exceed the standards), the instructor will approve the student for the flight test, and if performance during the flight test is within the standards, the student will pass the flight test.

It is not *easy* to perform within the standards, but the student is not going to be expected to perform to unreasonable expectations as the article implies.

Sincerely,

W.W.

32

No doubt the practice of selecting examiners who are affiliated with a flight school leaves the system open to the possible accusation of favoritism. Some schools even advertise the fact that they have a "staff examiner," the implication being that the student who enrolls at that school will somehow have an advantage when it comes to flight-test time. I recall one occasion, at an examiner meeting, when I turned to the examiner seated next to me and asked, "What's your bust rate?" He replied, "About 15 percent." When I asked how many of those he busted were from the flight school at which he was chief instructor, the answer was "None." This could mean that, if half his applicants were from his school, his bust rate for outsiders was a whopping 30 percent.

Even so, it is my personal belief that for every examiner who favors the graduate of the school where he teaches, there are at least two who "lean over backwards" to be harder on their school's applicants to avoid even the appearance of impropriety. On the whole, however, the vast majority of examiners are strictly impartial and evaluate each applicant just like every other one, regardless of where or by whom the applicant was trained. After all, the FAA spells out the standard to which the applicants must be held.

For many years the FAA selected examiners from the ranks of air carrier and corporate pilots, and I found fault with this. I believe that a pilot examiner should be a working flight instructor, someone who is actively involved in the aviation education environment. Many of the guys who spend their time charging through the sky in the high-altitude structure driving a jet have a real problem relating to the student pilot of very limited experience. Then there's the former military pilot with extremely limited experience in the real world of civilian flight training who is selected to be an examiner. This guy has a problem relating to the training environment and the civilian certification process.

Throughout the entire 17 years that I have been administering flight tests, I have always carried a student load (albeit a modest one—one primary, one instrument, and one CFI, plus an occasional multiengine student, glider, or seaplane student). I generally send my students to the FAA for their flight tests. I believe this policy of continuing to work as an instructor helps me do a better job as an examiner.

Besides, I really enjoy teaching, particularly beginning primary flight students. There's nothing I know of where the teacher gets as dramatic a demonstration of the results of his effort. When a flight instructor helps a primary student over one of the classic learning plateaus, you can see the student literally light up. "Look!" he says, "It works!"

Over the years I have seen many flight instructors "burn out." They simply get fed up with teaching, but it hasn't happened to me, and for several years I gave well over a thousand hours of dual instruction per year.

If the examiner can force the applicant to actually THINK during oral quizzing, it makes for a better evaluation than merely asking questions that call for rote memory-type answers. In other words, the idea is to probe for knowledge and understanding, rather than simple memorized answers to routine questions. For example, when I ask what's wrong with being over gross weight or out of the envelope fore or aft, I usually get the answer that it's unsafe. "Okay, what's unsafe about it? What kind of bad stuff can happen if you are overweight? Out of the envelope forward? Aft?" This requires the applicant to dig a little deeper into his store of knowledge to come up with answers, and I think it makes for a better, more complete examination.

33

There's no requirement that says an IFR pilot must slow down when flying to an assigned hold, but since the purpose of the holding pattern is to stop forward progress until the airspace up ahead can accommodate you, it only makes sense to go slower as one approaches the holding point. There are, of course, maximum holding speeds listed in the *Airman's Information Manual* [now *Aeronautical Information Manual*], but few training airplanes can achieve the 175-knot propeller airplane limit. Yet a great many instrument applicants go charging up to the fix and enter and remain in the holding pattern at high cruise speed. Although this is not disqualifying, it is certainly something I discuss with the applicant during his debriefing.

One reason for high-speed holding by the majority of instrument applicants is that they were trained in fixed-gear, fixed-pitch airplanes with reciprocating engines, and the difference between high cruise and a comfortable holding speed is so small that their instructors never bothered to mention that a pilot should slow down for a hold.

If you can slow down, you conserve fuel both in the hold and on the way to the holding fix. As soon as a controller calls me with an amendment to my clearance with a holding pattern as my new clearance limit, I slow down. If the holding fix is some distance down the airway, chances are I'll be cleared straight on through without having to hold at all if I can dawdle along and manage to kill enough time prior to reaching the fix.

An examiner has the opportunity to observe a number of such procedural operations that the applicant fails to perform wisely. Though not disqualifying, techniques such as slowing for a hold should be used and were apparently missed during training. The instructor certainly can't be expected to cover every little refinement. When these things show up on the check ride, I believe the examiner has a duty to call them to the attention of the applicant during the debriefing. This kind of teaching on the part of the evaluator (examiner) is okay. It's a far cry from instructing during the evaluation process or helping the applicant through one or another of the required tasks in the Practical Test Standards, a practice which is strictly forbidden. Let us remember, examiners are required to evaluate, and are not permitted to instruct.

A former student and applicant of mine who is now flying for a major air carrier told me that when he became a check airman the difference between a checker, an instructor, and a teacher was explained to him by his supervisor. A checker, he was told, says, "You bounced that landing!" An instructor says, "You bounced that landing because you retarded the power too soon!" And a teacher says, "You bounced that landing. Now, let me show you how to avoid doing it again."

I believe a good examiner has to be all three of the above. In critiquing the applicant after the practical test (whether the applicant passed or failed), the examiner should carefully, thoroughly, analyze the applicant's performance and explain just how it might have been better. If this is done in a kind and gentle fashion, learning is likely to occur. Of course, there is the occasional applicant who is not amenable to constructive criticism, who becomes defensive and wants to argue. He always attempts to fix the blame on some outside source. No matter what the problem is (or was), it's not his fault. It's hard to understand how this guy manages to learn anything at all. The majority of applicants, however, are more than willing; they are anxious to learn from their experiences. It is this kind who make the best pilots and who may well go forward with a career in aviation.

Most pilots say that each of their check rides has been a learning experience. I'm inclined to believe that what they really mean is that the debriefing after the ride was the learning experience, and not the ride itself. I know in my own case this has been consistently true. It seems that I've been taking check rides all my life, and I've learned something every time, but it has usually been during the debriefing.

We all know that a student (and we're all students at one level or another) does his learning on the ground. An airplane with the prop going around is an absolutely awful classroom. It is merely a learning tool with which we verify what we've already learned on the ground before the flight or during the debriefing after the flight.

To this extent, then, a check ride should be a learning opportunity for the applicant. During the test itself, as the FAA says, "There are no second chances." However, this doesn't mean that the examiner cannot give the applicant some helpful tips during the debriefing. And this is true whether the ride was passed or failed.

34

I haven't yet issued a recreational pilot certificate, but I recently had a private pilot applicant who was a perfect candidate. I operate at an extremely busy tower-controlled general aviation airport. In fact it is so active that we have two tower frequencies (the airport is divided right down the middle on an east-west line), one for each of the two parallel runways, and two ground control frequencies to handle surface traffic. As a result of being located at this field, other than a few applicants from outlying airports, most of the people I serve have been trained in a controlled environment.

Typically, appointments for check rides are made by the recommending instructor or the flight school where the applicant trained. But not too long ago, I got a call at home on a Wednesday evening from a student pilot requesting an appointment for a private check ride. I set it up for Friday.

At the scheduled time, two days later, I received a call from our tower chief requesting that I counsel the applicant when he arrived at my office. It seems he had called in on the south tower frequency, although he was arriving from the northeast. He was advised to enter a right downwind for Runway 27 Right and report on the north tower frequency. The next time he was heard from, he was midfield south of the airport, still on the wrong frequency (although it was technically correct for where he now was, it was not the frequency he was told to use and would have been wrong if he was where he was told to be).

When he finally arrived at my office, I used a chart and an airport diagram to carefully explain just what he had done.

After a marginally satisfactory oral (he met the minimum requirements), we went out to fly. He listened carefully to the ATIS, which was advising all departures to use ground control rather than clearance delivery, and then went ahead and called clearance delivery to announce that he was "ready."

After the controller got him straightened out, we taxied out to the run-up pad and he conducted a proper pretakeoff run-up. When he was ready to go, he called for takeoff clearance on the ground control frequency. He was advised to switch over to the tower. I had asked him to execute a soft-field takeoff, and when cleared to go, he swung out onto the runway, applied full power (without any flap application), charged down the runway until he was well above liftoff speed, and abruptly yanked the airplane into the air. I was completely dumbfounded, but, still curious to see what was coming next, I permitted him to proceed.

What came next was equally unusual. He leveled off at 600 feet agl and set off on his planned cross-country, still at full power! Meanwhile, the tower was frantically calling us, advising us of traffic off our right wing. I kept the traffic in sight and, after the fourth call from the tower, nudged the applicant with my elbow and said, "Hey, they're calling you!"

At that point I took the airplane away from him and we returned so that I could issue him his disapproval notice (pink slip). As he left my office to fly back to his home airport, I called the tower and warned, "Look out, here he comes!"

This nice man is in his late 40s and is an excellent candidate for the recreational pilot certificate. He will always be a fair-weather, Sunday-afternoon pilot who will never go more than a few miles from home and will take his friends for an occasional airplane ride. Of course, if he does decide to apply for a recreational certificate, his private written will be wasted, but so what? He can happily—and safely—exercise recreational privileges and derive much enjoyment from his hobby of flying.

01-22-95

Flying Mail

What is Howard Fried's logic in recommending the private pilot applicant for a recreational pilot certificate?

Although the applicant was attempting the private pilot practical test, Mr. Fried's story appears to indicate several requirements for the recreational pilot practical test also were failed: the safe and efficient operation of aircraft, airport and traffic pattern operations, collision avoidance, and maximum performance takeoffs and landings.

Both Mr. Fried and the editor don't admit the recreational pilot certificate has been an overwhelmingly rejected option. Recommending it or calling it an ideal starter license will only lose credibility.

Sincerely,

W.W., Jr.

Something I *don't* understand. RE: Howard Fried's column on training called "Eye of the Examiner." Always loved flying for the past 60 years (I am now 70), but the closest I've come to becoming a pilot was flying righthand seat in a PBJ (B-25) in the Marine Corps at Cherry Point in 1945. Then the war ended, and for myriad other reasons, I never continued my first love. But I digress. After reading the column, I wondered how Mr. Fried could allow this obviously unskilled man to take off to go back to his home airport? I suppose he flew the airplane in for the test, but after ignoring the four calls from the tower about traffic and just supposing what a threat he would be to other aircraft, how could the ruler allow him to fly? I could just see him getting confused in this TCA and flying in front of a 747 with a full load of people on board.

Marvin Hoffman

07 Dec 1994

To the editor,

I was shocked and appalled to read the article by Howard Fried in your December 94 issue. In "TRAINING: THE EYE OF THE EXAMINER," he described a student "pilot" who was so clueless that he should never be allowed near the controls of anything that leaves the ground. Mr. Fried told the story of this dangerous hopeful aviator by describing his inability to navigate, follow directions, answer or even tune a radio or control his aircraft. As a professional pilot who must daily share airspace with persons approved by Mr. Fried, I was amazed to see the article end with the student pilot being described as "safe" and deserving of a recreational license so he can go buzzing blindly about. That's about as safe for the rest of us out there as the trooper handing the keys to a staggering drunk and telling him to try and stay off the interstates. Why was he not grounded on the spot? I think Mr. Fried the examiner should re-examine his standards.

W.T.R.

35

Although the administration of a flight test is a very serious business—it is, after all, the "final exam" for the applicant for a certificate or rating—occasionally there is some occurrence, comment, or remark that can inject humor into the situation.

One such occasion came up several years ago. At that time, an instrument applicant was required to execute only one published approach, unlike the current requirement of all three of the standard approaches, and the applicant got to select the approach he wanted on the check ride. The particular applicant in question, after finishing an excellent oral, was preparing to go out and accomplish the flight portion of the test. I carefully explained just what he was to do, covering all the procedures and maneuvers. "Then, when we return for a landing," I concluded, "you'll execute one of the approaches to the published minimums. You get to pick the approach, so which kind would you like to do today?"

He unhesitatingly responded, "I'll take a visual!"

I'm sure this was designed to break me up, and it did. I don't think, however, that either a visual or contact approach was what the FAA had in mind when the Flight Test Guide (replaced by the Practical Test Standards) was written, and I insisted that he perform an ILS, NDB, or VOR approach, although one certainly has to give the fellow credit for trying. Incidentally, he elected to execute a VOR approach, and he did a fine job.

On another occasion an applicant coming from an airport some 40-odd miles distant arrived for his flight test just about an hour late. I had given up on him and had begun to believe that he had stood me up, when he walked in and announced that he was late because he had gotten lost on his flight over. One of our instructors overheard the applicant making this announcement. "For crying out loud," he said, "I wouldn't tell the examiner I got lost. Why didn't you just say you were late because you stopped off to see your girlfriend? Your examiner would probably be more understanding." By then it was too late to conduct the flight test, so, after carefully checking over his planning, I sent him home to try another day.

Then there was the private applicant who prepared a perfectly good plan for a trip to a destination some hundred miles distant on a magnetic heading of 255 degrees. When we took off, he promptly established himself on a heading of 190 degrees, and blundered along some 65 degrees off course. I let him go, hoping he would wake up, realize what was going on, and take corrective action. He didn't, at least not before we had proceeded almost 20 miles off course and were on the verge of entering a TCA (now Class B airspace) without a clearance. I had to terminate the test and disapprove his application.

We've all heard the adage "make a plan and fly your plan," but this can be carried too far, as exemplified by one private applicant I had a few years ago. After successfully completing the oral, this young lady and I went out to fly the airplane. She took off, established herself on the proper heading to fly the cross-country portion of the test, and climbed straight for a large cumulus cloud at about 2,500 feet. When we got to within 500 feet of the cloud and she showed no sign of leveling off, I asked her what she was doing. She replied that she had planned the trip for 4,500 feet, and by gum, she was going to fly her plan, even though in order to do so she would have had to plunge right through the clouds in her way!

The flight test is still a serious business. Most of these incidents, although tinged with humor, demonstrated a real lack of understanding of basic navigation or VFR rules.

36

There's an old saying among instrument flight instructors: "One peek is worth 10 hours of dual." I don't know what good that kind of cheating does in training, but it just won't do on a flight test. After all, who is the applicant cheating? Himself, that's who. And remember, we're dealing here with life and limb, not to mention potential extensive property damage. I cannot for the life of me imagine anyone wanting an instrument rating he did not earn, and earn the hard way. How can a pilot have confidence in his ability if he knows he cheated on a flight test?

I remember one particular instrument check ride where everything seemed to be going perfectly. When we got to the ILS approach, the applicant had the needles (localizer and glideslope) wired so well it looked like they were glued in place, right in the center of the donut. I don't know what it was that alerted me, but I suspected something was wrong. It was just too good to be true. Nevertheless, every time I glanced over, the applicant was intently staring at the panel. I checked the nav receiver to make sure he hadn't turned it off (in which case the needles would center themselves) but the radio was indeed on. Still, it just did not seem right. We were already well inside the marker and halfway down the glideslope when I unfolded a chart and covered the left side of the windscreen.

The airplane instantly went into a dance! He immediately got full deflection of both localizer and glideslope needles as we entered a

30-degree bank and about a 10-degree pitch-up. "Your airplane! You've got it!" the applicant shouted as he looked to me for help.

I never said a word about his attempt to cheat when I issued him his disapproval notice, but I did have quite a discussion with his instructor, who said he wasn't surprised. It seems the student had been bossy and very demanding throughout his training and had tried to tell the instructor how to train him.

Applicants, particularly student owners, willing to perjure themselves by making false entries in their logbooks can usually get away with cheating on the experience requirement, especially solo time.

But when it comes to the skill requirement, only an idiot would attempt to cheat by peeking out from under the hood. He's only cheating himself. If he can't keep the airplane upright without seeing out, how does he expect to survive in real clouds? It's almost impossible to deceive the examiner during the testing of any other flight skills, but on the instrument flight test it is often possible to see over or around the panel even with a view-limiting device in place. An applicant who chooses to cheat during an instrument ride is taking a chance with his very life, and worse still, with the lives of others.

Maybe the examiner won't find out what the applicant doesn't know, but it is absolutely certain that the applicant who peeks on his check ride will. One day he'll find himself in deep trouble. One day he'll blunder into heavy chop, with ice growing all over the airplane, and unless he knows what he's doing, he's going to lose it. When things get tough, you can't call a timeout, and the penalty is very severe.

If you want to fly on the gauges, be sure you have enough experience and skill—obtained under the supervision of a qualified instructor—to be really competent. Instrument flying in the real stuff is not particularly dangerous if you stay away from thunderstorms and out of ice, but it is challenging. It is also rewarding when done properly. I'll never forget a phone call I got at one in the morning from a recently rated instrument applicant who woke me up to say, "I just called to thank you. I just got in from a 260-mile trip on which I punched into the clouds right after liftoff and never saw the ground again until I broke out on short final, 200 feet above the ground with runway lights on both sides of my nose."

January 26, 1995

Dear Mr. Fried,

I'm a 50-year-old senior high school science teacher working on my private pilot's license. I think "Eye of the Examiner" is always the first thing I read in each new edition of *Flying*. I found your article in the February '95 issue of particular interest.

I'm not surprised at your story of the IFR student attempting to cheat on his check ride. As a teacher with 20+ years experience, I have seen it frequently, and it is becoming more and more accepted. No longer is cheating considered wrong; it is considered creative problem-solving. Within the last three years, I have actually received notes from parents giving permission for their son/daughter to copy other student's work. Last year, a student, who also worked for the school as a teacher's assistant, had access to and photocopied the final exam for my class. He then sold the photocopies to other students. When caught, there were no consequences for their actions; all students received full credit for their test results, and the offending assistant remains a student assistant today. I had no say in the matter; I'm just the teacher, not the school administration, who makes the final judgment in such matters.

As I see it, the problem of cheating exists because there is little if any repercussions for cheating within our educational system or society. I applaud your February article and the disapproval notice given the student. I sincerely hope you were not subjected to giving the same student a second check ride at a later date.

Sincerely,

Charles L. Kay

February 13, 1995

Dear Mr. Kay:

The editors of *Flying* have forwarded a copy of your letter of January 26th to me, and I feel compelled to answer it personally. I get copies of all mail concerned with my column, "Eye of the Examiner" and I answer all those which have a point to make, particularly the fan mail (and I even get some of that). Those which bitch merely for the sake of bitchery don't get an answer, nor do those without a return address, or on which the return address is illegible.

Over the years since I started the "Eye of the Examiner" column I've received several letters that made me feel good, but very few that have touched me to the extent that yours has. Your letter was doubly heartening because in the same mail I got a copy of a letter sent from an irate reader in Maryland suggesting that I be fired by *Flying* for empathizing with the poor guy I wrote about in the November issue. The "Eye of the Examiner" generates far more of that kind of mail than it does the favorable kind, and I treasure the good ones. Thanks again.

Today's attitude toward cheating (and other unethical activity) seems to be: there's nothing wrong if you don't get caught! Your analysis carries this one step further; and if you do get caught, so what? Nothing will happen to you anyway! It's a shame we live in an era and society where this situation prevails.

By the bye, I don't remember whether or not I got that guy back for his recheck, but I think he went to another examiner, being too embarrassed to come back to me.

Best wishes for a long and happy career in aviation,

Howard

37

I cannot speak for any other examiner, but for myself, the responsibility of being a pilot examiner and issuing certificates and ratings is a frightening burden. It is a responsibility that weighs heavily, and no doubt many if not most examiners feel the same way. I live in abject terror of the time when I issue a certificate to an applicant and read his name in the paper the next week. It hasn't happened yet, but just as I admit that someday I might land with the gear up, so do I recognize that I may be confronted with this terrible event one day.

When one thinks of the time, energy, and emotional pitch an applicant puts into reaching the level at which he meets the examiner for his check ride, one can't help but hope he does a good job and demonstrates the competence required for his certificate or rating. Most examiners, I suspect, are like me and truly enjoy issuing a certificate or rating to an applicant who has done an exceptionally good job on his flight test. To see the applicant go forth with a smile on his face and a new certificate or rating in his pocket is a distinct pleasure. On the other hand, it's a real bummer to see the disappointment in the expression of the applicant who had to be turned down. An FAA inspector, addressing an examiner meeting, once said, "If it bothers you to bust an applicant ya shouldn't be an examiner!"

My reaction to this was, "Balderdash!" It bothers me a whole lot every single time I have to turn down an applicant. Disregarding the investment in money he has made, the emotional letdown when an applicant busts a check ride must be extreme. I enjoy seeing a well-prepared applicant perform all aspects of his or her flight test perfectly. The ones the examiner agonizes over are the marginal applicants who just manage to squeak through, barely meeting the requirements of each task or, perhaps, very slightly exceeding the tolerances, with semivalid excuse for their failure to do so. You know what I mean: "The wind blew me over," or "A gust came up just as I was flaring to land." It is these, the ones who could go either way, that drive the examiner up a wall, and most of us are inclined to pass them on through. Of course, the FAA maintains that there is no such thing as a marginal applicant. They either meet the standard, or they don't, but we all know that this is simply not so; some meet it better than others. No two applicants, both fulfilling all requirements of the PTS, are going to perform to the same level of competence. One may give the examiner a letter-perfect ride, while another may barely get by.

While the marginal applicant may give the examiner fits, the good, clean bust is another matter. The applicant who does something so outrageous that it is very clear he was not prepared for his check ride, the one who knows just what he did wrong and when he did it, these don't give me the problem that the marginal ones do. But I feel sympathy for them, too. They've put in just as much time, energy, money, and emotion to get to that point as has any other applicant, and it is a difficult thing to have to issue disapproval notices and disappoint them. On more than one occasion I've had applicants who failed, pass on a subsequent recheck and come back some weeks or months later to tell me that it was a good thing they didn't make it the first time. They recognized the need for a bit more training and were grateful for having had to return to their instructors for it.

The designated pilot examiner is not the only person in the training and certification community who carries a burden of responsibility. The certified flight instructor is another individual who has a heavy burden of responsibility, as does the pilot in command of any flight on which passengers are carried. But unless you've been there, you cannot know and appreciate the feeling of responsibility that weighs on the examiner.

38

A unique relationship exists between the certified flight instructor and the pilot examiner. Unfortunately, this liaison is not always what it should be. Ideally, these two parts of the certification process should exist in a spirit of cooperation, but occasionally they find themselves in an adversarial position. I know not how other examiners feel, but personally I respect and admire the flight instructor who shows enough interest in his trainees to call me to discuss their performance after they've been evaluated. As an instructor, whether an applicant I recommend passes or fails, I want to know how well I prepared my student for his check ride.

A few years ago there was an instructor who, rather than sending his applicants in cold to make the appointment for their check rides, would lead them in by the hand and introduce them to me. During the flight portion of the evaluation, this fine young instructor would monitor the radio and as soon as we landed would be there to sit in on the debriefing. His attitude was, "What can I do to give you a better one next time?" This young man so impressed me that when the flight school where he was working went belly-up, I hired him to teach at my school.

His interest stands in stark contrast to the guy who ran a one-man flight school and who, when I had occasion to call him to discuss the performance of one of his applicants, would say, "I don't want to talk about him. He's already got his certificate. Let me tell you about the next one I'm about to send you."

My answer to this was invariably, "Please don't. I don't want to know anything about his skill from you now. I need to see for myself just what he does." The guy was unhappy with my policy, believing that if he could brief me on each of his applicants before I met them, I would be better able to evaluate them, or perhaps he was attempting to prejudice me on their behalf. I'm not sure which. But I do have a suspicion.

On a regular basis I have scheduled and held instructor meetings at all the schools from which I get applicants. We go over the Practical Test Standards and discuss just how the instructors can better prepare their applicants to meet the published performance requirements. This helps the beginning instructors learn what's expected, reminds the experienced instructors, and encourages them all to do a better job.

The truly effective flight instructor stands at the very pinnacle of the aviation professions. But although he is arguably the most important individual in the entire aviation community, he is not looked upon with the respect he deserves. Until the flying community elevates the instructor from the bottom rung of the ladder of aviation professionals to the level his contribution warrants, communication between examiners and instructors will continue to suffer. Many examiners, particularly those who are not actively involved in the education process, look down on the instructor as some lesser being who is to be tolerated rather than admired and respected. This is no doubt because there are many flight instructors who are just marking time, using their instructor positions as stepping stones in their own careers while they acquire the experience they need to make themselves more attractive to corporate or air-carrier employers. And they are doing so at the expense of their students! Their attitude is reflected in the product they turn out, and the result is what the examiner sees at check ride time. And it is on the students' performances that the examiner bases his opinion of instructors.

There is, however, hope on the horizon in the form of the efforts by the FAA and others to improve the status of the flight instructor. But raising the level of professionalism will continue to be a difficult, if not impossible, task unless and until the instructors themselves understand the heavy responsibility they carry and respond with the dignity their profession deserves.

As a representative of the Administrator, the examiner is in a unique position to encourage the dedicated CFI and instill a sense of responsibility in those lacking these essential qualities.

39

Flight schools and indeed flight training in general are plagued with the problem of dropouts. In extreme cases this can happen even at the very end of the training process. In 17 years and more than 4,000 flight tests administered, I've twice been confronted with the unique situation of a check ride that never was. In both cases, the applicants, who had completed their training, been recommended by their instructors, and scheduled the check ride, canceled the appointment and never took the test to acquire the certificate. Although it's very rare, I've heard of this happening from other examiners as well, and I have to wonder if it isn't an extreme example of "checkitis" or exam jitters.

In the first of my two cases, an applicant for a Single Engine Seaplane rating on his pilot certificate had completed his training and been recommended by his instructor. At the scheduled time—on a Saturday morning—the applicant met me at my office at the airport, where we accomplished the oral portion of the practical test. We then got into his car and drove the 6 miles or so to the lake where the airplane was normally anchored.

When the applicant and I arrived at the lake for the flight test, we discovered the airplane wasn't there. It seems the owner had taken it away for the weekend without bothering to let anyone know it wouldn't be available.

The fact that the oral had been completed but the flight portion of his check ride would have to be postponed for a day or two so upset the applicant that he refused to reschedule his ride, and to this day, some 10 years later, he still does not have his seaplane rating.

The other case was even more unusual. The woman had completed her training and been recommended by her instructor for the flight test. She actually showed up at the appointed time but announced that she couldn't take her check ride. I like to think I am neither superstitious nor unreasonable, and I certainly have nothing against anyone's beliefs, but her excuse for not taking the private pilot practical test gave me pause. She explained that her biorhythms weren't right and her stars weren't lined up properly for an important activity that day. She also refused to reschedule the check ride.

There may very well have been another, hidden, reason for her refusal to acquire the certificate for which she was qualified. It seems that both she and her husband were simultaneously taking flight instruction and there was an element of competition between them. I suspect that, in deference to her husband, this woman didn't want to finish first and embarrass her husband, whose training was not quite completed, and whose pride she believed to be at risk. As it turned out, her husband, who was encountering severe problems learning to fly, dropped out. As a result of his failure, his wife never took her own check ride even though she had completed the training and been recommended.

This business of one spouse holding back to give the other an opportunity to catch up or move ahead is not altogether uncommon. I've also seen partners and friends defer to one another out of a sense of politeness, but never before or since to the extent that a student refused to take that final step. I find it difficult to understand how anyone who has invested the time, effort, and energy (not to mention the money) to reach the final stage of pilot training could then simply give up and not take the final exam. It's got to be a virulent form of checkitis.

It's only normal for applicants to show up for a flight test with some degree of nervousness or anxiety, and this gives the examiner one of his biggest problems. The examiner wants to see the applicant's best effort, and he certainly can't see that if the applicant is all tied up in knots with a huge case of nerves. Some applicants are so uptight that they are utterly incapable of expressing themselves. In one extreme case, a private applicant, a young medical doctor, showed up for his test in such a state of nerves that he had to excuse himself and go to the gentlemen's lounge and toss his cookies prior to the start of the check ride. Once he got that over with, he settled down and performed very well.

Don't let "checkitis" check your progress toward a goal you've worked hard to achieve. Once you've completed your training and secured your instructor's recommendation to take the practical test, you've earned the right to demonstrate your ability to an examiner. The examiner is not looking for a reason to fail you but is only attempting to confirm your instructor's conviction that you are qualified to share the airspace with the rest of us. Once you've successfully completed the training and gotten the signoff, you owe it to yourself—and your instructor—to take that final step to become a certificated pilot.

40

All of us know at least one guy who has all the answers, and if you don't believe it, just ask him. You know who I mean: The guy who's frequently wrong but never in doubt. His way is the only way of doing something, all others are wrong. Unfortunately, Mr. Know-It-All could be a pilot, an aircraft mechanic, a flight instructor, or even a pilot examiner.

I've known two examiners over the years who fall into this category. Fortunately for the aviation community, neither is an examiner anymore. One retired and the other lost his designation because he refused to comply with the published standards. Whereas most examiners who deviate from the PTS err on the generous side and, playing Santa Claus, give away certificates and ratings, this guy insisted on substituting his own, different, and higher standards for those of the FAA.

You all know the type. He's another version of the student pilot who hangs around telling the ATPs how to fly an airplane. We had one of those for a while at our flight school, and he was virtually unteachable. We've also seen the instructor who did things a little differently and who honestly believed that the only right way was his way, in spite of the fact that everybody else did it by the book. It is a sad day for aviation when one of these guys becomes an examiner.

I know of one case where an examiner took a private applicant out for a check ride at night, in the rain, in submarginal VFR conditions and had to file IFR to get back in—in an airplane that wasn't certified for IFR flight. The examiner said he could better evaluate the applicant under those conditions, and if the student wanted to go, who was he to say no? That's similar to the instructor who dispatched a student pilot on a cross-country flight with tornadoes popping up all over the area. The instructor defended his action by saying, "How else can they learn if they don't go out and see for themselves?" The FAA suspended the instructor's certificate for that one, and the damn fool went down and argued that he'd done nothing wrong, claiming that the best kind of teaching is to let the student gain experience on his own. Another instructor I know insists on demonstrating (or having his student demonstrate) a single-engine takeoff during the course of training for a multiengine-airplane rating, even in some of the marginally performing twins used for training multiengine pilots. No curriculum I've ever seen includes this maneuver.

Just as some instructors insist on doing things their own way, so do some examiners. But, as the name implies, the Practical Test Standards (PTS) were published to standardize flight tests. What I'm suggesting is that when you take your next check ride, be sure the examiner stays within the parameters of the Practical Test Standards. Most, but not all, do. In one case an applicant for an instrument rating flight test was busted because he didn't have an IFR area chart. There's nothing in the regs that says you have to have one, but the examiner required it. A pilot is supposed to have all appropriate charts for any given flight. But an area chart for an instrument flight? Come on.

Each examiner can, of course, set his own weather minimums, and many refuse to fly unless the weather is substantially above VFR minimums. Others will administer a flight test in any weather that's good enough to get in all the tasks in the PTS.

The Practical Test Standards spell out exactly what is expected of you. If you get an examiner who asks for some maneuver or procedure that isn't in the PTS, don't hesitate to tell him it's not required. If he attempts to hold you to a higher standard than the PTS, tell him what the standard is (the PTS spells that out, too), and if that doesn't reach him, complain to the local Flight Standards District Office of the FAA. The FSDO will have an inspector ride with you, and if you meet the standard, you will be issued the certificate or rating. The examiner no doubt will be counseled, and if he persists in exceeding the requirements of the PTS, he will not be an examiner too much longer.

41

Some examiners have come up with their own unique techniques or "tricks" to test an applicant, but in using some of these techniques it is possible to create a potential emergency or even a disaster. Some examiners, for example, cause an actual emergency by surreptitiously reaching down and turning off the fuel valve in a Cessna 150 to institute the simulated forced landing due to engine failure on the private flight test.

I know of other examiners who pull the circuit breaker for the landing gear in complex airplanes where this is possible. They then wait to see if the applicant checks gear-down during the landing approach. This practice is particularly dangerous, because the examiner might be distracted at the same time as the applicant and they could very well wind up with that short step down that results from a gear-up landing. And it's not uncommon for the same event to distract both people occupying the front seats of an airplane.

Another test technique that I believe is potentially dangerous is sometimes used on glider check rides. The wing struts on many training gliders are attached with bolts with a small hole through which a safety pin is inserted to secure the bolt. One examiner I know removes the safety pin and places it in his pocket as a test to see if the applicant will notice its absence when he accomplishes the preflight walk-around inspection. All that's required for disaster to strike is for the examiner to be distracted and forget he has the pin in his pocket when the glider takes off.

On the other hand, there are many legitimate techniques that an examiner may use to determine the level of preparedness of the applicant. One I frequently use checks the applicant's knowledge of night flying without the necessity of having to go out with him after dark. In assigning the cross-country planning portion of the private test, I'll ask the applicant to plan a trip to an airport some hundred miles away and tell him or her that we will lay over there until 10 o'clock that evening. We will then proceed to another airport, perhaps 50 or so miles from the first destination. The second airport I select is a nontower airport with pilot-controlled runway lights. What I'm looking for is to see if the applicant is well-enough trained to check runway lighting availability and control in the *Airport Facility Directory* and note it on his trip planning log. It is surprising how many don't.

When going over the trip plan of those who haven't noted on their trip log that they must key the mike so many times on such and such a frequency, the following conversation usually occurs:

"That airport has lights, does it?" I ask.

The applicant, checking the chart and seeing the "L," responds, "Sure does!"

"Are the lights gonna be on when we get there?"

The applicant, noting the asterisk on the chart, shakes his head. "No. I have to turn 'em on."

"Ten-thirty tonight is no time for you to look out and see a large dark space and then, with a flashlight clamped in your mouth, be checking the chart while the airplane goes into a dance. I'd have been a whole lot happier if you'd noted the frequency and the number of clicks on your trip log."

This kind of thing, while possibly leading the applicant into a self-imposed trap, is perfectly legitimate. Of course, the failure to include the requirement for pilot-operated lighting in the flight log does not necessarily result in a bust, but it does challenge the applicant to think. Some may call this sneaky and a trick, but I call it a fair means of probing for knowledge and preparation. What do you think?

There are lots of similar techniques examiners use that some applicants and instructors deem to be unfair. They're under the impression that examiners are just looking for an excuse to turn down an applicant. In reality, nothing could be further from the truth. What the examiner is doing is simply testing to determine if the applicant is ready to assume the awesome responsibilities of pilot-in-command.

42

Every once in a while something I write touches a very sensitive nerve.

For example, one reader took profound exception to my comment that a majority of flight instructors, without overtraining or "milking" their students for additional training and the costs of that training, prepare students to a higher standard than that required by the Practical Test Standards. I pointed out that when a student is trained to hold altitude and heading precisely, then passing a check ride where tolerances are allowed is a cinch.

The reader claimed that this kind of training places unreasonable demands on the student—that in fact, instructors who insist on perfection are driving students away.

I recall vividly back in 1943-44, when I attended CIS (Central Instructor School) at Randolph Field in the old U.S. Army Air Corps, learning the principle that if an instructor demands perfection, he gets it, and if he allows any tolerance, the student will exceed it. Over the years since then I have found this concept to be an especially valid one.

The reader advocated training the primary student to maintain altitude within 300 feet and gradually progressing down to the minimum standard of the PTS (plus or minus 100 feet) and then stopping. My own experience has been that when an instructor permits students to wander within the given parameters of the PTS, they'll likely wander outside those limits. If I ask a student to fly at 3,500 feet plus or minus 100, I get anything between 3,200 and 4,000. Likewise, if I call for a heading plus or minus 10 degrees, I am likely to get more like 20 degrees from the assigned heading. And the student thinks this is okay. On the other hand, if I ask for 3,500 exactly, or a precise heading, I get exactly what I'm looking for, right on the money.

The same principle applies to ground training. If a student is expected to be perfect, to answer all the questions correctly and get 100 percent on all his practice written tests, then the real thing is easy. We have always followed this practice at our school and the result has been nothing short of spectacular. Of 550 graduates from our ground school classes a few years ago, there was a grand total of three busts on the written.

The reader maintained that meeting the standard of the PTS is not easy, and asking for more is unreasonable. I agree it is not easy. Nobody ever said it has to be easy. Early on I was told that flying an airplane is the easiest thing in the world to do and the hardest thing in the world to learn, and that may be true. But I don't believe it is any more difficult to learn to do it precisely than to learn to do it imprecisely. In any event, it sure is a lot easier to pass a flight test if the applicant operates the airplane with precision.

Let's not forget for a moment that the PTS standards are absolute minimums. I'm fairly sure most of us don't want to share the airspace with minimally performing pilots.

Subj: The April "Eye of the Examiner"
Date: 95-04-17 22:00:23 EDT
From: Psyfly
Posted on: America Online

Howard Fried has done it again, arousing the ire of some of your readers for his view of good flight instruction style. This time he goes way back to his "vivid recollections of the old U.S. Army Air Corps" to justify his immediate personal demands for perfection. There were many more determined candidates than aircraft, and the alternative was the infantry. Time was of the essence. Under those conditions, one could get away with the "kick ass and take names" approach. Being mean, demanding, unreasonable, and picky was worn as a badge of courage by the likes of Mr. Fried, and that style probably might have been a comfortable fit with his personality, thereby becoming the "best" method, of course.

Today that unfortunate CFI attitude, combined with a lack of understanding of how to maximize the rate of learning with today's flight student, has driven off many a potential addition to the ranks of general aviation pilots. Too many CFIs have not had training in how to work with their students to keep them interested, pleased, and achieving higher and higher levels of skill. I'm sure Mr. Fried finds those words as profane to the corps of hard-bitten, steely-eyed examiners. Fun? Who ever said learning to fly should be fun. It has to hurt to be good, right?

For that matter, why place immediate and unreasonable demands on the student when they are paying by the hour and want to enjoy the process, unless it's to feed the ego of the instructor (examiner)? Perhaps there is something very wrong about setting progressively higher but achievable goals, thereby helping the student to succeed and go on. Perhaps Howard can comment on this.

Do I sound like I had a Howard Fried type as my first instructor? Yes, I did, and I fired his ass and got someone who could teach. He almost caused me to drop out of the thing I had longed to do since childhood, to fly airplanes. Unfortunately, not enough beginners have lived long enough to take that point of view. Too often, they just quit and blame themselves. And, the number of active pilots goes down each year.

It's not a matter of high standards. Aviation rightly demands them. Hold a student to +/− 40 feet of altitude if you wish. What counts is helping students to get to that level of proficiency without losing them.

Whew! Do I feel better now.

D.R.

Subj: Re: The April "Eye of the Examiner"
Date: 95-05-27 19:23:27 EDT
From: EYEOFEXAM
Posted on: America Online

Dear Mr. R_____:

Over the years, my column, "The Eye of the Examiner," has raised a good deal of controversy, which, by the way, is very welcome. It seems that there is someone, somewhere, ready to take violent exception to virtually any statement I make.

The column to which you refer generated several letters, but you should know that they are running 19 to 2 in favor of the technique which I espouse.

You should also know that as an instructor I have never been mean or unreasonable. Demanding yes, mean and unreasonable no. As for driving people away from aviation, please be advised that in many hundreds, even thousands, of students I have trained, my personal drop-out rate is less than two percent. So much for losing potential aviators. How many other instructors do you know that can claim such a low drop-out rate? I must be doing something right!

It is too bad you "fired the ass" of the demanding instructor and hired one who permitted you to direct your course of training and let you get away with sloppy flying. Some day you may come to regret having had a wimpy pussycat for a primary instructor. If striving for perfection "almost caused you to drop out," perhaps you should have done so.

I'm sorry if this answer to your complaint seems harsh, but the subject is one about which I feel very strongly.

Good luck, blue skies and sunshine,

Howard

Subj: February "Eye of the Examiner"
Date: 95-06-29 13:27:10 EDT
From: Psyfly
Posted on: America Online
Howard Fried
"Eye of the Examiner"
Flying Magazine
6/18/95

Dear Howard: (part 1, since this is too long for Online). Check for part 2.

While reading *U.S. Aviator* (another magazine), I discovered the problems you have had with FAA personnel. I'm very sorry that I wrote what I wrote when I wrote it, and I apologize. Your plate is already too full, and I didn't mean to heap on more.

I read your replies to my comments very carefully, and I can see how one needs to communicate clearly. The English language is not always sufficiently exact. Our interchange has forced me to clarify what I was trying to say and eliminate the unnecessary emotional stuff.

Having knocked around in aviation for a few years, and having had some relatively fresh experiences in entering aviation as an avocation, I have seen and experienced a number of practices which, in my view, erode the life energy and growth of general aviation. Many of these practices appear self-inflicted by too many unskilled businessmen running FBOs to many poor instructors because they can fly but they have not been trained to deal with people, and archaic habit patterns and outdated practices passed down from generation to generation of aviators and the FAA. Most recently, we see the FAA foolishly adding to general aviation problems by outrageous use of faulty research to justify new medical requirements they must need for political or other self-serving reasons.

My response to you was on the problem of instructional skills and procedures of CFIs. I remain convinced that because budding airline pilots need so many hours, they turn to FBO instruction in 152s and Tomahawks to build hours. Almost all are really in aviation to fly airplanes, not to deal with the problems of teaching demanding skills to mostly recreational pilots, both men and women, who strive for achievement, fun, excitement, and perhaps the realization of dreams of flight. CFIs tend to be flyers, not teachers, and there is a big difference. Only occasionally does one come along who can do both.

The future of general aviation lies with those who fly for pleasure. And most of them learn to fly safely, if they persevere in the face of today's requirements. I recognize that flying is an open-ended and difficult set of skills. One can never be finished with acquiring the skills of safe flight. There is too much to know and experience. I think we both agree that high ultimate skill standards are necessary, and that the student must develop the habit of excellence in order to fly safely. To quote my original letter, "Demand +/− 40 feet altitude, if you wish." The important issue then is "What is the best way to bring students along to that high standard?" As I understand your views, the CFI needs to set high standards from the beginning. I would call that making ultimate goals clear about where you want to get, and I think that students will accept those standards because they want to live to a ripe old age.

Subj: February Issue, "Eye of the Examiner"
Date: 95-06-29 12:31:36 EDT
From: Psyfly
Posted on: America Online
Howard Fried, Part 2 from Psyfly

However, we may differ after that, for I believe that once the student has the ultimate goals in mind, they learn quicker and better by focusing on one aspect of flight at a time, preventing overload. And when they fail, the most powerful move is to encourage, not demand. These principles are borne out in Air Force research findings. By and large, general aviation students need encouragement, considerate correction, patience, support, and recognition of small achievement, even though performance at that time does not reach ultimate standards. Those words may seem mamby-pamby to the old-timer, but they are basic motivational techniques for any human being, even for the best and toughest of our pilots who must constantly learn new aircraft and new procedures. Too many CFIs are impatient, bored, or downright rude in their correction of student errors, and they fail to see the value of recognizing good performance. In short, they are often poor teachers who discourage too many budding pilots. If there were better teachers, you would see finer pilot skills and many more students ready for your examination. At risk of really getting into trouble, the best instructors I now see in general aviation are women, who fly very well and seem to be better equipped to teach. How's that for blasphemy?

As for my flying skills, I am known as a very conservative and dedicated pilot who holds a very high standard of performance for myself. I have taught safety skills to over a thousand commercial pilots, almost all of whom rate my instruction very highly. Like you, I love aviation, flying, and would like to help preserve general aviation for the future. I also try to tell it the way I see it.

Best wishes in your struggle with the Feds.

Psyfly

Subj: Re: February Issue, "Eye of the Examiner"
Date: 95-06-29 19:33:36 EDT
From: EYEOFEXAM
Posted on: America Online

Basically you and I are in general agreement. Unfortunately there is a
built-in flaw in aviation education for which there doesn't seem to be
a solution. I am referring to the fact that the ranks of flight instructors
are filled with ambitious young aviators who are marking time while
they acquire the experience to make themselves attractive to the corporate air carrier employers, and THEY'RE DOING IT AT THE EX-
PENSE OF THEIR STUDENTS! One was recently heard to say, "I'm
only doing this until I can get a real job flying heavy iron!"

What these jerks fail to realize is that the highest pinnacle to
which an aviator might aspire is to be a truly great PRIMARY flight instructor! I believe this is the highest calling in aviation. After all, there
isn't an astronaut who stepped on the moon, there isn't a high-time
senior captain operating one of those flying condominiums across the
big puddle who didn't start with a primary instructor who taught him
the habits he has carried with him all his flying life!

For more, check your e-mail.

Howard

Subj: Re: February Issue, "Eye of the Examiner"
Date: 95-07-08 08:51:50 EDT
From: EdwardM191
Posted on: America Online

Amen!

A friend of mine once commented (he was, in fact, my instructor at the time, speaking of influences that last a lifetime) that we've got this whole aviation thing bass-ackwards. The way it should work (assuming airline aspirations) is 1) training, 2) right seat of small commuter/corporate/freight, 3) captain of same, 4) right seat of major airline, 5) captain of same, 6) THEN instruct.

Subj: Re: February Issue, "Eye of the Examiner"
Date: 95-07-08 18:12:54 EDT
From: EYEOFEXAM
Posted on: America Online

Your instructor sure knows what he's talking about. Another thing that's bass-ackwards is the pay scale. However, this will never be corrected as long as we have time builders and part-timers who like to fly but can only do it at someone else's expense. (Nothing wrong with either category so long as they're dedicated TEACHERS.)

43

The majority of letters I get indicate I have mistakenly conveyed the impression that inspectors and examiners are constantly lying in the bushes waiting to pounce on any insignificant little error on the part of the applicant and to use it as an excuse to bust him. Apparently, I'm the worst offender. This couldn't be further from the truth. There are at least three people who actively want the applicant to pass his or her check ride—the applicant, his instructor, and the examiner. The instructor wants to maintain his record, the applicant wants to feel proud of his accomplishment, and the examiner wants to pass him along so he doesn't have to recheck him. I know I do.

Believe me, it's a lot easier to pass an applicant than to fail him. Every bust has to be justified by matching the applicant's action (or lack thereof) to a specific pilot operation in the Practical Test Standards (PTS). A bust entails more paperwork than a pass, and we know how everyone, including inspectors and examiners, loves paperwork! And remember, the examiner has to fly the recheck with anyone who busts—always a nuisance.

With one or two extremely rare exceptions, almost nobody I know derives any pleasure from handing out a Disapproval Notice (pink slip). Examiners only do this when it is required by the regulations. It is the regulations that fail the applicant, not the examiner. Of course, in the larger sense, it is the applicant who busts himself, by failing one or more tasks within one or more areas within one or more pilot operations of the PTS. The Practical Test Standards are designed to guarantee that only well-prepared applicants find their way into the airspace.

We all want the pilots with whom we share the airspace to be good, competent, and safe. And the only way to ensure this is to see that every applicant meets the PTS for the certificate or rating for which he is applying. There may be "Santa Claus" examiners who pass unqualified applicants, but with today's system for designating and training examiners (and inspectors, too) they have to be extremely rare. Personally, I do not know, or know of, a single examiner who would knowingly turn an unqualified applicant loose in the airspace.

The one area where an otherwise apparently qualified candidate could slip through the system is in judgment—or the lack thereof. Since judgment is both subtle and very difficult to define, it is virtually impossible to evaluate. Occasionally an applicant will do something during the check ride that displays extremely poor judgment. When this happens, the examiner or inspector must look for one of the pilot operations in the PTS to which he can tie the bust. Not only hard to evaluate, judgment is next to impossible to teach. However, by setting a good example, an instructor can help to train his student in the area of judgment.

Within the framework of the PTS, each examiner has favorite areas he tends to emphasize. I know one examiner who goes into great depth on the subject of aircraft performance. Personally, I'm an absolute nut on the subject of weight-and-balance. In almost every accident report I've studied, and I've studied a lot of them in depth, weight-and-balance is a factor. It may not be the determining factor, but it is a factor. Often it is the cause of the accident, and when it is, the accident is almost invariably fatal. Consequently, in oral quizzing, I want the applicant to not only know it is dangerous to be over the maximum allowable gross weight or out of the envelope fore or aft, but why.

When it comes to passing the flight test, it is all a matter of preparation. The properly prepared applicant is guaranteed to pass. Remember, nobody is looking for an excuse to bust you, rather the examiner is looking for an excuse to pass you. You can count on it!

44

Eighteen years ago, when I first became a Designated Pilot Examiner (DPE), the inspector who recommended me said, "Remember, the FAA giveth and the FAA can taketh away." After 17 years of service as a DPE, I was shocked when, with that warning only a vague memory, the local District Office did indeed taketh away and decided not to renew my designation. I can't go into details here because I'm appealing the decision, but it has been a good reminder that an examiner serves at the pleasure of the FAA; the designation is discretionary with the designating District Office.

When I was first designated as an examiner, the process was simple. In our district you didn't ask to be designated; you had to be chosen. If there was a need for an additional examiner in the district, the General Aviation Operations Supervisor (then called a Unit Chief) would ask the Principal Operations Inspectors for recommendations. He would then look at the records of the instructors who were recommended and make a selection based on the pass/fail performance of their students.

Way back then, the selected instructor would be called in, given a copy of the examiner's manual, a complete set of the old Flight Test Guides (since replaced by the Practical Test Standards), a few pads of Temporary Pilot Certificates and Disapproval Notices (pink slips), and be told, "This manual tells you what to do and how. The Test Guides set the standards. Issue Certificates to successful applicants, and Disapproval Notices to unsuccessful ones. Bless you, my son, go forth and give flight tests!"

A couple of years later the FAA set up a program of standardization for DPEs. A team of three inspectors from Oklahoma City called the PEST (Pilot Examiner Standardization Team) visited every District Office (GADO or FSDO) in the country and put on a four- or five-day clinic. Every examiner in the country was required to attend. Every two years since the program was inaugurated, the team completes the circuit with a completely new program. Today, the clinics have been condensed to a single day, but attendance is still compulsory. The idea is that no matter where or from whom you take a check ride, you will be held to exactly the same standard and the outcome will be identical. That's the intent. How it works in practice may be another matter entirely, but at least a solid effort is being made.

An examiner's designation is for private, commercial, and instrument privileges in any single-engine airplane. For any other airplanes (seaplanes, gliders, and each specific make and model of twin), the examiner must have a separate letter of authority. The additional authority is granted—if a need in the district exists—by the examiner training an applicant and having that applicant tested by the FAA; by the examiner taking a check ride in that make and model; or, more usually, by the examiner being observed by an inspector while administering a flight test in the make and model.

Normally, an examiner renews his designation annually by the end of his anniversary month. At that time, he visits the local District Office where the record of flight tests he has administered is reviewed, he is instructed in any new procedures, and he takes a ride with an inspector. I'm not sure whether the ride is supposed to be a test of his ability or more of a standardization ride in which he is shown standard techniques.

Sometimes, as it did in my case, the District Office declines to renew an examiner's designation. Of course, in order to revoke or refuse to renew a designation, the FAA should have a valid reason. I'm challenging the FAA's justification and I'll let you know how well I think the appeal process works in a future column.

45

When all the oral testing and flying are said and done, whether an applicant passes or fails a check ride depends finally on whether or not he meets the performance levels of the PTS (Practical Test Standards). But even so, the examiner or inspector can't help but be influenced by the attitude, actions, and appearance of an applicant.

One of the most important things an applicant can do to show he's serious about the test is to be prompt for the appointment. It doesn't hurt to even be a little early. It has always been surprising to me to see how many applicants show up late for their flight test. When an individual is tardy for something as important as a flight test, the evaluator can't help thinking he isn't addressing the situation with the seriousness it deserves.

What the examiner is looking for is a well-prepared applicant. So another way for an applicant to favorably impress the examiner is to have the paperwork, particularly the application form, properly filled out. It should be neat and above all accurate. For example, the examiner will be negatively impressed with the applicant's ability to follow instructions if he has entered his height in feet and inches when the form clearly states that it wants this number in inches only. Any such discrepancies have to be corrected before the examiner forwards the paperwork to the FAA, and the examiner isn't likely to be pleased if he has to correct the mistakes of the applicant and the recommending instructor. I've even had more than one applicant come in for a check ride without an application. The excuse offered in each case was that he didn't know one was required. That's not a good way to start the oral exam.

When an applicant presents himself to the examiner, his overall attitude is extremely important. An air of quiet confidence—without a trace of cockiness—makes a favorable impression. There's nothing wrong with being nervous; examiners expect virtually all applicants to show some signs of nervousness. But while it's perfectly normal to be anxious, demonstrating an extreme lack of confidence in one's ability is not.

If you really want to impress the examiner, simply knock the oral portion of the practical test right out of the park. Remember, if you're so well prepared that you come up with concise, correct answers to the examiner's questions during the oral quiz, you'll convince him you really know your stuff. At this point he'll have already made up his mind that he is working with a superior applicant. Then, later on in the test, if your performance is something less than perfect, for example if one or more of the flight maneuvers are not quite up to standard, the examiner will be forced to question his own judgment if he wants to mark you down. After all, you've already demonstrated you know your business.

We all like to think we have good judgment, and nobody, particularly a pilot examiner, enjoys admitting he made a mistake in judgment. Therefore, he'll likely start looking for excuses for your poor performance. A gust of wind blew the aircraft off the centerline; the glare on the windscreen caused you to flare a bit too high. Whatever it was, it could not have been your lack of skill that caused the bad landing. The examiner knows this because he's already made up his mind that he is working with a good applicant.

Trust me, if you apply the simple principles outlined here, your next check ride will be a piece of cake. Remember, all you have to do is be well prepared, show the examiner you know your stuff, and fly the aircraft to the standards of the PTS.

46

Just how far wrong may an applicant go before an examiner terminates the flight test and disapproves the application? In my own case, I'm favorably impressed by an applicant who makes a timely self-correction. If an applicant starts on a maneuver the wrong way but then catches himself or herself before it goes too far and proceeds to do it right, I'll give him full credit for that particular task. But how far is too far?

If an applicant wanders off course on the cross-country portion of the private pilot check ride, I'll let him go quite a way before giving up. I want to give him a chance to catch himself and get back on course. "Quite a way" could be as much as 8 or 10 miles.

On the other hand, if an applicant, in the performance of one or another of the ground reference maneuvers, starts off by making a wrong wind correction and doesn't correct it within about a minute or so—remember, that's a long time when you're traveling 2 miles per minute—I would probably terminate the ride at that point.

If an applicant starts to flare for landing a bit too high and an alarming sink begins to develop, I wait until the last possible second to see if he'll apply a bit of power to put a cushion under us before I grab the controls. An applicant who demonstrates that he's been taught how to correct a bad landing—or rather the start of a bad landing—shows me more than an applicant who might have been lucky and greased one on.

If an instrument applicant catches himself after starting to make an improper entry into a holding pattern, I won't mark him down for it—as long as he doesn't violate his assigned airspace. Remember, although the PTS clearly requires an applicant to use the recommended entry procedures, in the real world, nobody cares how it is done just so the pilot doesn't violate the protected airspace.

Most examiners and inspectors don't care if an applicant is a little high on a nonprecision approach. But they feel very differently if he gets below the published minimums. This also applies to the initial portion of a published approach. If the applicant is slightly above the depicted altitude, nobody cares. Just don't get lower than that number! Of course, there's no tolerance beyond the three-dot limit on an instrument approach once the fix is passed.

If, while recovering from an unusual attitude on instruments with a view-limiting device, an applicant makes a false start and it isn't corrected almost immediately, I'll end it right there. In such a situation, there is virtually no room for error. This is particularly true of a spiral dive, the infamous graveyard spiral.

Once, when I was conducting a multiengine check ride, the applicant forgot to retract the landing gear after the initial takeoff. I waited to see how long it would take him to realize he hadn't raised the gear. He climbed to 3,500 feet, leveled off, and set up the airplane for cruise with the wheels still hanging out in the breeze. I thought surely he'd realize something was wrong after he configured the airplane for cruise and found we were going a lot slower than we should have been.

He didn't recognize his mistake until I finally asked, "Shouldn't we be going faster than this?" Normally I wouldn't have let him get that far. I would have terminated the test as soon as he had climbed well away from the airport, but I was curious to see just what he was going to do and when.

How far will an examiner let an applicant go before calling a halt to the proceedings? Most examiners will permit quite a bit of leeway. In an effort to be fair to the applicant and give him every possible opportunity to meet the standard, examiners will wait to see if he'll make a timely self-correction. Making a mistake isn't necessarily disqualifying, providing the applicant is able to recognize the mistake and to take the appropriate corrective action.

47

Good as it is, the certification process is an imperfect system. Although the vast majority of applicants who acquire certificates and ratings earn them, once in a while an unprepared applicant slips through the cracks.

It's easy to understand how it happens. An instructor recommends an applicant who is less than well prepared and, in sampling his skills, the examiner neglects to check the one or two specific tasks in which the applicant is weakest. As a result, a pilot who is really not qualified becomes the holder of a certificate or rating that authorizes him to engage in activity for which he is not adequately prepared. He has slipped through a crack in the system, and he may be a menace to himself and others in the airspace. While it is the responsibility of the recommending instructor to see that his applicants are properly prepared, it falls upon the examiner to weed out those who are not.

Sometimes the best thing that can happen to an applicant is to bust his flight test. Occasionally a student is overconfident and feels the instructor is holding him back unnecessarily, so he pressures the instructor to recommend him. In extremely rare cases I've had instructors come to me and tell me the applicant they're sending in should fail his check ride for his own good. In other words, instead of looking for excuses to pass the applicant, I should look for an excuse to bust him.

When a flight instructor expects an examiner to bust one of his applicants, what he's really doing is asking the examiner to be the bad guy—to do the instructor's dirty work for him. The instructor knows the applicant isn't really ready, but he sends him in anyway, expecting him to fail.

In the case of most certificates or ratings, if a pilot who isn't really qualified slips through, that's just one pilot, but there's a situation where this isn't so. If an unqualified applicant makes it through the Certified Flight Instructor flight check, the result can be disastrous. He can do a bad job of training several generations of pilots and thus turn literally hundreds of bad pilots loose in our airspace. A frightening thought, isn't it?

Unfortunately it does happen. And the really pitiful thing about it is that such an instructor's primary students never know the difference. When we were students, we thought our instructors were some kind of gods—not only could they fly, but they could teach us to fly. If, perchance, we had a bad instructor, we had no way of knowing it. And the situation is no different today. Most students know only what their instructors teach them, and they usually have no reason to question what they are being taught. The student rarely has a basis of comparison unless he is fortunate enough to see more than one instructor at work.

I've said before, and I say again, the most important individual in the entire aviation community is the primary flight instructor, for it is from him that the student pilot acquires the habits that he carries forth throughout his entire career as a pilot.

Of course, the student can make the instructor look good or bad. The best instructor in the world can send up a marginal student, and pass or fail, the examiner thinks to himself, "Boy, that guy had rotten teaching." Then up comes a natural student, one who teaches himself how to fly while his instructor merely sits there and prevents him from committing suicide, and the examiner thinks, "Boy, this guy had great instruction." Even so, after evaluating several examples of the product of a given flight instructor, an examiner can pretty much tell how good he is.

48

Many examiners—and probably most pilots—believe the most important check rides are those for advanced ratings and certificates, particularly the instrument rating. In fact, several examiners have told me they are tougher in holding their applicants to the standard for advanced ratings than they are with the private.

But an FAA inspector once told me that he felt the private is the most important check ride a pilot ever takes. After thinking about it, I'm convinced he's probably right.

As Lincoln said of the common man, so it is with the private pilot—there are a great many more of them than any other grade of certificate holder, so it is extremely important they be well-grounded in the basic skills of flying.

We must keep in mind that the FAA's Practical Test Standards (PTS) are bare minimums, and the private pilot applicant who just squeaks by is a long way from being the accomplished pilot he will become with experience. Unfortunately, there's simply no way to cram experience. It can't be hurried but only comes with the passage of time—more time than most students get along the way to their instructors' recommendation for the private certificate.

The private pilot applicant who performs the best is the one who excels in executing the fundamentals. There are really only four things an airplane can do: climb, descend, turn, and fly straight-and-level. Any maneuver an airplane is capable of performing is one or a combination of these four fundamentals. And the pilot who executes these maneuvers with flawless perfection is the truly great pilot, at least in terms of being an airplane manipulator.

To be really good at any motor skill, such as airplane manipulation, takes repetition and drill, repetition and drill. And once acquired, this sort of skill must be kept current with still more repetition and drill.

It has often been said that the private certificate is a "license to learn," and there is an element of truth in that statement. The new private pilot is presumed to have met only the minimum skill requirement for the certificate. Thereafter his skills are expected to continue to improve. But if he doesn't keep practicing the fundamentals, it will never happen. It is not the number of hours in the air that count but how those hours have been spent. If every single flight is not a learning experience, the pilot is wasting a golden opportunity.

The importance of acquiring and maintaining skill in the performance of the fundamentals of flying simply cannot be overemphasized. But to be a really great pilot, the factor of good judgment must be added and this is even more important than being skillful at manipulating an airplane.

49

In addition to being medically qualified, applicants for all grades of certificate (except student) and for some ratings must satisfy the administrator that they have the requisite aeronautical knowledge, experience, and skill to be entrusted with the privileges of the certificate or rating sought. The experience requirement is demonstrated by logbook entries attesting to the training and practice. The skill requirement is met by the demonstration of ability to an inspector or examiner on a check ride.

The knowledge requirement is usually thought of as being satisfied by a passing score on the appropriate written examination. However, this is not necessarily the case.

The flight test or check ride is intended as a practical test of not only the applicant's skill but also his knowledge. The oral quizzing continues throughout the test, and the examiner's responsibility extends beyond how well the applicant performs to what he knows and understands. And just because an applicant does well on the written, there is no guarantee that he really has the knowledge required to entitle him to the certificate or rating.

I vividly remember an applicant from a nearby flight school who came to me for a private pilot flight test several years ago and presented me with a written result showing a score of 100 percent. (On average, I would see about three 100s every two years.) After going over his qualifications, I assigned him a cross-country trip to plan. When he finished his planning we got down to work. After 35 minutes of vainly attempting to drag one single correct answer out of him, I started writing down the questions and his (wrong) answers. Finally I gave up and, after I had the guy sign the paper with the some 20-odd questions and his wrong answers, sent him off with a disapproval notice.

Ten minutes later he was back with his instructor, who had absolutely come unglued. The instructor was unable to comprehend the fact that someone who hadn't missed a question on the written could bust the oral and never get to the airplane. The instructor was absolutely enraged—mad at me, not the applicant. He ranted and raved in the public portion of our offices until I demanded that he and the applicant step into my private office, where I closed the door, sat them down, and attempted to calm the instructor.

Sitting in my office with the two of them, I turned to the applicant and again asked the same questions I had written down and again I got the same wrong answers.

The way I figured it was that the applicant had taken the written almost two years earlier and had no doubt forgotten much of the material, if indeed he'd ever really known and understood it. The CFI had then made the mistake of assuming that anyone with a written score of 100 wouldn't require any preparation for the oral portion of the practical test.

The lesson here is that any instructor who makes an assumption is falling into a trap. Although this might seem understandable, it is still the instructor's responsibility to see that his or her applicants are prepared for the practical test.

An area of particular danger for a flight instructor is when he inherits a student-in-progress from another instructor. Even though certain procedures and maneuvers have been signed off in the student's logbook by the previous teacher, the new instructor must check for himself, probably at the risk of engendering resentment on the part of the student, who is concerned with the economics of the situation. An instructor simply cannot assume anything.

50

It has been said that there are nine different FAAs, since each region makes its own policy; in some cases the FAA even goes so far as to have each District Office establish policy within the district. For example, when I first became an examiner, and for the next few years, the fees that examiners charged for check rides were standard. Each examiner went his own way as far as rechecks were concerned, but there was an established fee for initial check rides, and everybody charged the same fee. Then one day, at the annual examiner meeting, the District Office Manager announced that this policy smacked of price fixing, and we should each set our own fees.

Of course, the natural law of the marketplace went into effect. If any examiner set his fees too low, all the rest of us would be mad at him, and if any examiner charged substantially more than the average, he wouldn't get any business. So it all sort of evened out anyway, but there was still a range of fees being charged. Meanwhile, in several other FAA districts, the policy of a standard fee schedule for all the examiners remained in force. In fact, it is my understanding that this policy is the one most generally followed throughout the system. (Although the fees vary widely around the country, they are the same within each district.)

As far as I know, the fees for reexaminations are left up to the individual examiner everywhere. If an applicant has to come back for a second or third try, or so on, many examiners charge a full fee each time. Others charge their hourly rate for retesting, and what the ap-

155

plicant pays depends upon how long the check ride or portion of the check ride takes.

My own policy was to charge half of my regular fee for a recheck, whether we had to repeat the entire test or merely a single task. Obviously this policy was unfair to the applicant who only had one or two items on his disapproval notice and a bargain for the one who had to do everything over again, but from my viewpoint it all came out in the wash and seemed to be the simplest way of handling the situation. Of course, in those cases where 30 or more days had passed between the first bust and the recheck, I would charge a whole fee for the second check ride, for in those cases a complete practical test is required, just as if it were the original check ride. As far as I know, this is the policy followed by all examiners everywhere.

It is infrequent that an applicant will bust a flight test for the same certificate or rating more than once, but it does happen. On the recheck, most examiners only test the applicant on those tasks that were unsatisfactory on the previous ride, but it must be remembered that all the tasks of the Practical Test Standards (PTS) are fair game. If the examiner should observe, on a subsequent flight test, that an applicant's performance of a task previously performed satisfactorily is not up to the PTS, he is required to put the applicant down. In such a case I'm sure the examiner would get a vigorous argument, against which he had better be prepared to defend himself.

After the required 30-day lapse following a second bust, the requirement for a complete retest exists, no doubt to prevent a truly unqualified applicant from slipping through. I heard of a case in which an instrument applicant busted a check ride by performing six tasks unsatisfactorily. On his first recheck he got two of them right, on the next try the examiner tested him on only the four remaining tasks. It took that poor fellow four tries to get his instrument rating, and one week to the day after he received his rating he had a fatal accident in IMC. Had the examiner required that fellow to do a satisfactory job on the complete test when he was rechecked, he would probably never have gotten his instrument rating, and he might be alive today.

51

Several readers have complained that I devote an inordinate amount of space to writing about flight test busts. They say my emphasis has been on the negative aspects of check rides. That's true. The study of aviation safety—by its very nature—is largely devoted to the study of accidents, for it is from the misfortunes of others that we learn; and so it is with flight tests.

It is from the mistakes of others that we can learn what to avoid. Instead of merely knowing what to do, knowing what *not* to do can be of equal importance. Many of the mistakes applicants make during the course of taking the practical test for the Private Pilot Certificate are related to really basic, fundamental aspects of flying safely.

For example, one of the most common errors I've observed in the more than 4,000 check rides I've given over a 17-year period is the large number of private applicants who fail to clear the area prior to the entry of any maneuver in which a substantial loss of altitude—or speed—may be expected, such as stalls. On the whole, today's students aren't taught to look around outside the aircraft as much as they should. People who wouldn't dream of turning into an intersection with their automobile will blindly roll their airplane into a turn without so much as a glance in the direction of the turn. They simply bury their heads in the cockpit, staring at the instrument panel, as they start the turn. Not good.

Another place where applicants—and not just private applicants—are frequently not as alert as they should be is in the airspace around airports. This is, of course, where traffic might be expected. Many of my applicants, when cleared for takeoff by the control tower, roll right out onto the runway and start the takeoff roll without checking to see if there's anyone on final for the runway they're about to enter. They are depending on the tower controller to look out for them. Personally, I want all the eyeballs I can get watching out for me, but I know I still have to look out for myself. Somehow we acquire a sense of security when we know a controller is watching us. But that sense of security is often false. The bottom line is that we're responsible for seeing and being seen ourselves. So I'm always looking around. Pilot applicants should be, too.

Another of the fundamentals that gets overlooked with some degree of regularity is basic airspeed control and the use of various power settings. In the days when we flew around in Cubs and Champs, we used three power settings: full power for takeoff and climb, idle power for descent and landing, and cruise power for all else. Since the introduction of the gradual power-reduction technique for operation in the landing pattern, the applicant is expected to be able to exercise total control over the machine in a wide variety of power settings. This requires training and practice in flight at a variety of airspeeds from cruise to minimum controllable airspeed, and many applicants are lacking skill in this area.

Instrument applicants frequently ignore a most basic fundamental: Always have every needle on the panel point to something useful. A substantial number of instrument applicants often permit some of their expensive avionics to be lazy and just occupy space rather than doing something positive. By this I mean, for example, while tracking an airway, they will often permit their number two VOR to do nothing, instead of tuning it to a station off to the side and keeping track of their position along the road.

It's certainly valuable to learn from your own mistakes—but it's less time-consuming and costly if you can learn from someone else's.

52

Just as there is a great deal of difference in the way flight instructors teach a specific maneuver or procedure, so are there differences in the way examiners want to see pilots perform the tasks required of the PTS. If the pilot candidate doesn't perform to the examiner's satisfaction, the flight test is a bust.

I get quite a bit of mail asking about these differences, as well as whether examiners have a quota with respect to their pass-fail rate. A typical letter was one from William Black, who wondered whether examiners had quotas, since "cops are often accused of having to produce X number of tickets or they are on the carpet." He went on to point out that "Most police forces try to have reliable, sensible cops. But [one] would be a fool to fail to recognize that a sadistic one gets in uniform occasionally. After all, an examiner wields a lot of power."

As to quotas, no. Examiners do not have a quota—although the FAA keeps telling examiners at meetings and clinics that they expect to see a 15-percent bust rate. I recall an incident at an examiner meeting at our local FSDO. At the end of the meeting as we were filing out—after having been told several times that the FAA was looking for a 15-percent bust rate—the inspector in charge of the meeting passed out pads of temporary pilot certificates and pads of pink slips (disapproval notices). The examiner ahead of me in line requested several pads of temporary certificates.

"And how many pinkies do you need?" the inspector asked.

"Oh, about fifteen percent," the examiner replied.

The system is really self-policing. If an examiner busts too many applicants, instructors will quit sending him or her any more applicants. On the other hand, if an examiner is a Santa Claus type, literally giving away certificates and ratings, the FAA will ultimately jump all over him.

While the vast majority of examiners try to be fair and impartial, reader Black is correct that occasionally a sadistic one does slip in. He's the guy who holds the opinion that he's the only one qualified to be an aviator and virtually no one else can measure up to his own high standard.

At least as bad, and somewhat more common, is the inconsistent or erratic examiner. I've known some who are easy or tough as the mood strikes them. They will pass an applicant today for the same thing they busted one for yesterday. We like to believe an examiner is going to be consistent in his rulings. But in spite of a very intense effort by the FAA to standardize the practical testing of aviators, as long as human beings are conducting the examinations, there will always be differences in how they are administered. No two people can be expected to react in exactly the same way to any given situation.

I've also known examiners who, after a string of passes, figure they'd better bust the next applicant who comes in just to make the record look good and to keep the feds happy. This may also happen on the subconscious level without it being the result of deliberate thought.

Whatever an evaluator's failure rate, if you as an applicant can perform to the standards of the Practical Test Standards, you shouldn't have any trouble. If you do fail a flight test and you aren't sure why and believe you met the standards, make the examiner or inspector explain why you failed and what would have been acceptable performance. The PTS is very specific and that's the only standard you're required to meet.

53

There are some kinds of flight tests that can only be administered by FAA Aviation Safety Inspectors or Flight Standards District Office Operations Inspectors. I have in mind airman check rides for Part 121, 125, and 135 operators, Designated Pilot Examiner flight checks for original designation and designation renewal, special medical flight tests, and the infamous 609 ride.

It is section 609 of the Federal Aviation Act of 1958 that authorizes the FAA to recheck a pilot to determine if he or she is still competent to exercise the privileges of his or her certificate and ratings. The dreaded 609 ride is normally used as a post-accident or post-incident check and is intended to examine the phase of flight involved. For example, after a landing mishap involving a moderate crosswind, a pilot might be asked to demonstrate his ability at landing with a crosswind. In that instance, the 609 ride makes sense. But there have been occasions in which inspectors have abused their power under the 609 rule.

Although the wording of section 609 would seem to indicate that any pilot might be asked to demonstrate his competence to perform to the level of his certificate and ratings at any time, for any reason, or for no reason at all, the National Transportation Safety Board has repeatedly ruled that the FAA must have just cause to require a pilot to take a 609 ride. The question then becomes one of what is a just and proper reason.

I know of an instance in which a flight instructor mouthed off at an inspector, enraging the inspector to the extent that he demanded the instructor come to the FSDO and take a 609 ride to see if he deserved to be an instructor. And I've heard of similar cases of abuse of power by other inspectors.

Flight instructors are particularly vulnerable to having their competency brought into question, and perhaps this is as it should be. On the theory that the instructor is responsible for whatever his student does, whenever a student pilot is involved in an accident or incident, the competency of the instructor seems to be the issue. Of course this is sometimes valid.

I recall an instructor who had a terrible record in terms of getting his students to pass the private certification flight test. He professed to be a conscientious CFI, and he sought the counsel of all the examiners in the area. But he apparently ignored what he was told. This instructor went shopping in an unsuccessful attempt to find an examiner who would pass his product. Finally, his record (something like 80 percent of his students busted their check rides) came to the attention of the FAA, and he was called in to the FSDO to discuss the situation. The FAA discovered that he had been operating as a primary flight instructor with a Class II Medical Certificate that had expired more than two years previously, and it took that fellow four more trips to the FSDO (after renewing his medical) and a lot of intensive work with an FAA General Aviation Operations Inspector (he required two ground and two flight sessions) to get his privileges restored. Even so, to the best of my knowledge, that particular CFI never again attempted to teach. Fortunately for the rest of us, he gave up flying altogether.

When an individual pilot somehow slips through a crack in the certification process it is bad enough, but in the case of an unqualified CFI, the effect can be spread among all the pilots with whom he comes in contact over who knows how many years.

The 609 ride, as unfair as it can seem when improperly required, is still one of the few ways we have of identifying problems—and implementing fixes—before they can cause more serious damage.

54

It seems as if I've been taking check rides all my life. At one point I was taking at least four flight tests a year with the FAA. Usually I don't suffer from checkitis. I psych myself up for the ordeal by telling myself that I'm going to go out and show the man how I fly, and if it isn't good enough, then I don't deserve to pass. This attitude adjustment works for me. It lets me relax and fly the airplane as well (or badly) as I normally do. I don't go in all uptight.

I did bust one ride. It was on another six-month check in a twin. The inspector cut an engine when I was halfway between the marker and the runway on an ILS approach. I took immediate action to keep the aircraft under control and going straight, but I did get a full-scale deflection of the localizer needle. I called a miss and, still under the hood, started climbing out. The inspector gave back the failed engine and we took vectors around for another shot at the approach. Again he cut an engine when we were almost at the threshold. But this time, as I saw the needle going off scale, I thought, "I can catch that," and I started to turn back to finish the approach. As soon as I did, I knew I'd blown it and busted the ride. It was quiet in the airplane for a while on the way back, then the inspector said, "Howard, we won't say anything about this. You come back tomorrow and we'll do an ILS, okay?"

I told him I had nothing to hide. I'd screwed up and that was all there was to it. When I got back to my office I announced to a room full of people, "Well, your Old Dad just busted a check ride!"

One of our flight instructors said he'd hate to be the next applicant to face me, since, now that I'd busted a check ride, it would, no doubt, be easier for me to bust an applicant. I'd hate to think that's true, but it is an interesting thought.

It is my considered opinion that the attitude of the applicant has a great deal to do with the outcome of a check ride. With the occasional rare exception, almost no examiner takes any pleasure from disapproving an application, but if the applicant does fail to meet the standard of the PTS, it wouldn't be doing him a favor to pass him.

The thing to bear in mind is that a disapproval notice is not a failure—it's a deferment. It merely delays the awarding of the certificate or rating, and only for a relatively short time. It gives the applicant, who wasn't yet quite ready, a chance to get a little more training and practice so he or she can demonstrate his or her ability to meet the standard of the PTS. The best way to look at it is to ask yourself if, 10 years from the day you receive the disapproval notice, it will make any difference whether you got the certificate or rating on that date, or whether you acquired it a few days later. Remember, you didn't fail, you just postponed the rating.

55

In a past "Eye of the Examiner" column, I exposed a few techniques used by examiners (and instructors) to distract applicants (or students) in an effort to determine whether or not the applicant or student would remain focused on the primary task of flying the airplane or permit himself to become so involved in solving a minor problem that he would let the airplane get away from him. The number of things that can be done by way of distraction is almost limitless. For example, the FAA recommends that the applicant may be asked to look out and count the number of rivets along the second rib in the left wing of the airplane. This, I think, is a bit obvious.

Much better is the creative examiner who comes up with something more realistic. An example of this kind of distraction might be for the examiner to suddenly shout, "My gosh, did you see that airplane that just flew a few feet over (or under) us?" The applicant is almost guaranteed to respond, "Where is it?" as he looks frantically around, perhaps leaving the airplane to its own devices rather than continuing to maintain control. Of course any time an examiner or instructor desires to induce vertigo in an applicant or student, all he has to do is, while the victim is under the hood (or otherwise with a view-limiting device in place), put the airplane in an unusual attitude (a well-established spiral dive is preferred), place his pen or pencil on the floor, and ask the victim to pick it up. If the applicant (or student) leans over and bends his head as he goes for the pen or pencil, he is almost guaranteed to get vertigo.

Reader Chris Hulen tells of the time his instructor, while working on ground reference maneuvers (low and slow), claimed to have been bitten by either a snake or scorpion and was moaning in pain. The instructor begged his student, Chris, to locate whatever it was and prevent additional damage. By this time he claimed to have been bitten again. Of course the entire scenario was an artificial attempt to see how the student would react. Chris managed to keep the airplane under control while checking under the seat for whatever had bitten his instructor, and thus he passed the test.

This scenario isn't really too farfetched, for I was present at a small sod airport in Pennsylvania when a Tri-Pacer made an un-scheduled landing. The pilot exited the airplane (tumbled out, rather than making a normal exit). He ran a few feet away and called for help. It seems a copperhead had fallen from the headliner onto his lap while in flight. Fortunately, the pilot wasn't bitten (the reptile was no doubt as startled as the pilot). The story ended when the airport op-erator pulled the snake from the floor of the airplane with a rake, and it slithered away.

Another such event occurred when a large female rat turned the upholstery in the rear seat of a Skyhawk into a maternity ward and nursery. The pilot in this instance was not so fortunate. He, too, made an unscheduled landing, but only after having been bitten by the mother rat.

In both of these cases the pilot was alone at the time. I guess it re-ally pays to carefully preflight the interior of your airplane as well as the outside and engine compartment, particularly if your airplane has been parked outside for an extended period (and the airport is built on the landfill over a former dump, as is Cleveland's Burke Lakefront Airport).

These inflight distractions are entirely different from the tricks some instructors and examiners use to catch an unwary student or applicant failing to execute a proper preflight inspection. You know, the tape over the pitot tube or static port (or both), the obstructed fuel vent, the missing fuel cap, etc., all of which have been used since the Wright brothers started it all. It may be recalled that in a previous "Eye" column I mentioned the fact that as we taxied back from the flight portion of the practical test I would ask the applicant to drop me off so I could start the paperwork while he secured the airplane. I would then attempt to deplane while the engine was still running, hoping the applicant would refuse to let me do so. Rather than a dis-traction, this was a test of the applicant's readiness to assume com-mand authority. Many applicants, particularly private applicants, were too timid to refuse to let me out before the propeller stopped.

56

Flight instructor applicants have always been required to explain each maneuver and procedure as it is taught. In fact, great emphasis is placed on the instructor applicant's ability to explain why each element of each lesson is important in the performance of the maneuver. On the flight instructor check ride, the "explanations" are at least as important as the ability of the applicant to demonstrate the maneuver.

Now, since the Practice Test Standards (PTS) have replaced the old Flight Test Guides, the standards for all certificates and ratings require the applicant to explain each item, and after five years of experience with the PTS, we're *still* not seeing it.

The objective of each task as published in the PTS starts out "To determine that the applicant exhibits knowledge by explaining the elements . . ." This new requirement is part of a greater scheme. Formerly, the flight test was administered in two distinct parts. First came an oral examination, followed by the check ride itself. Now, however, it is all one practical test that includes oral quizzing as well as observation and evaluation of the actual performance of the task. Thus, the "oral" continues throughout the entire test.

Even under the standards of the Flight Test Guides, examiners have always had the duty as well as the authority to continue to probe the applicant's knowledge throughout the entire test experience, but rarely would an applicant fail the oral portion of the test after he and the examiner actually got in the air. Now, under the Practical Test Standards, it is much more common for this to happen.

The reason for this lies in the fact that the applicant is given much greater opportunity to display a lack of some essential knowledge. After first talking himself into it, he just may keep right on talking until he has talked himself back out of it!

Once again: The objective of each task in the PTS commences, "To determine that the applicant exhibits knowledge by explaining the elements . . . ," and it means exactly what it says—the applicant is expected to be able to explain the elements of each procedure and maneuver. By the time an applicant presents himself to the examiner (or inspector) for his flight test, he has been—or should have been—exposed to the appropriate PTS for quite some time, and he should certainly be aware of the fact that explanations are expected of him. However, in the "real world," most examiners very rarely get to see an applicant who is really prepared to explain *what* he is doing as he performs a maneuver, let alone *why* he is doing it.

This tells us that the instructor didn't do his job of properly preparing his applicant. Remember, it is the instructor upon whom this deficiency reflects, for if an applicant is properly prepared, there's no excuse for busting a flight test. What the examiner is really doing is checking the instructor's work.

In order to "demonstrate knowledge by explaining," the applicant should volunteer the explanation without the examiner having to probe for it. When we achieve this state, we will truly be meeting the standard as spelled out in the Practical Test Standards as published by the FAA.

Appendices

A

Pilot examiner program

The FAA pilot examiner program has come under attack by the popular press recently, in both the *New York Times* and the *Wall Street Journal*. It has been alleged that because pilot examiners, whose duty is evaluation, are also instructors, whose job is teaching, the examiner cannot be unbiased. These articles argue that because evaluators charge a fee for their services, they are motivated to pass unqualified applicants for fear that if they hold all applicants to the standard instructors will not send them any more applicants. The articles also charge that if evaluators work at a flight school, they are motivated to pass the graduates of their own school to keep up the school's enrollment.

These attacks go on to cite specific abuses of the testing procedure by specific examiners, and some of the cases cited are horror stories indeed, particularly one regarding an examiner who sat in his office and watched out the window while the applicant flew the pattern and landed, after which the examiner issued a certificate attesting that the applicant had completed all the required tasks for the private pilot certificate. Another incident involved an ATP examiner who decided to forego the test because the weather that day wasn't very good but who issued the ATP certificate anyway after a brief oral examination.

The examiner's certificate of designation states that the United States Government has placed special trust and confidence in the integrity, diligence, and discretion of the examiner and has found that he has the necessary knowledge, skill, experience, interest, and impartial judgment to merit special public responsibility. It is, however, well known that not all examiners have all of these attributes. Occasionally one slips through a crack who lacks one or more of these sterling qualities. We are all human beings, and no doubt, at least to some extent, we are influenced by our own life experiences, and this influence is reflected in our actions and judgments.

The article that appeared in the *Wall Street Journal* quoted an examiner who had evidently lost his designation for lack of activity as an examiner. Each examiner must conduct a minimum number of flight tests annually to keep up his or her designation. This particular former examiner complained to the *Wall Street Journal* reporter that he didn't get any applicants because the flight instructors in his area were afraid of the fact that he tested to the standard and had an unusually high failure rate. He implied, of course, that the other examiners do not give a comprehensive flight test up to the standards of the Practical Test Standards and that the instructors are seeking easy examiners who will pass anyone who comes along.

This just is not true. Far and away the busiest examiner in one FAA district has the highest bust rate in his district, his fee is the highest around, and he has a reputation for being a very tough examiner. Yet he gets all the business he can handle; he administers more than 300 flight tests per year. The reason, no doubt, is because he also has a reputation for being scrupulously fair—he's the same miserable S.O.B. toward all applicants. Another reason this examiner enjoys so much flight-test activity is because he makes himself available when the applicant is ready. The time to give a practical examination is right now, when the applicant has his or her graduation certificate or instructor's recommendation in hand, before he or she can either go stale or work up a state of nerves. The examiner wants to see the applicant's best effort, and he or she can't see that if the applicant is all tied up in knots with "checkitis."

The same *Wall Street Journal* article complained about the built-in conflict of interest that seems to exist when an examiner owns or is employed by a flight school whose graduates he or she tests. No doubt there is some validity to this point. On the other hand, just as there might be examiners who go easy on applicants from their flight schools, there are surely at least as many examiners who bend over backwards to thoroughly test the graduates of the school with which they are affiliated. In addition to being concerned that it would look bad if they passed all the applicants of their own schools, these examiners are interested in seeing that their schools turn out the very best pilots they can. Liability considerations aside, most instructors want their applicants to be thoroughly tested to the Practical Test Standards (PTS). Most applicants want to have a complete flight test for their own sense of well-being.

The program the FAA now has for training and retraining the designated pilot examiners is excellent. As recently as 20 years ago, when a need for an examiner became apparent, the local FAA District Office looked over the list of qualified flight instructors in the area and selected one. The district office then called the instructor in to the local General Aviation District Office (GADO) or Flight Standards District Office (FSDO) and, in essence, handed the instructor a copy of the Examiner's Manual, a set of the old Flight Test Guides, a few pads of Temporary Airman Certificates, and a few Disapproval Notices (pink slips), and told the instructor, "This manual sets out the limits of your authority. Follow it. These booklets spell out the standards to which you should test applicants. Follow them. Issue temporary airman certificates to successful applicants and disapproval notices to unsuccessful ones. Bless you. Go forth and administer flight tests."

The process is quite a bit different today. For starters, the screening process is much more thorough. Then there is the training and retraining, which continue indefinitely. In 1978 an outstanding program for designating, training, and standardizing pilot examiners was created. Directly responsible to Flight Standards at the national headquarters of the FAA in Washington, but housed at the FAA Aeronautical Center in Oklahoma City, is a small group of superior educators called the P.E.S.T. P.E.S.T. stands for Pilot Examiner Standardization Team. When it was first formed, this group put together a program using the latest and best educational techniques available, including the psychodram and the very effective use of video. Then they took this show on the road, and within two years they had put on a five-day clinic in every FAA District Office in the world. Attendance of all existing pilot examiners was required. After this initial go-around, the program has been completely revised and updated every two years, and every single pilot examiner must attend. These programs are designed to update the training and standardize examiners within three days, or 24 hours of work, but they are now sometimes completed in two 10-hour days with four hours of credit for the precourse study guide (homework!).

Newly designated examiners must travel, at their own expense, to Oklahoma City and attend the original five-day course prior to starting work as an examiner, and thereafter they must attend the revised program every two years when the team visits the individual districts. Also, each new examiner must take a check ride with an FAA General Aviation Operations Inspector in his or her own district prior to starting operations as an examiner. All examiners, both old and new, are required to fly with an FAA inspector annually to renew their designations. These flight checks are more in the nature of standardization rides than pass-fail flight tests. The examiner is expected to demonstrate the procedures and maneuvers called for in the various Practical Test Standards for which he has authority as the FAA wants and expects to see them performed. While acting in their official capacity as Designated Pilot Examiners, examiners are representatives of the Administrator of the FAA. They are really working as employees of the government. Additionally, on a workload-permitting basis, all examiners are supposed to be observed during the administration of a flight test one or more times a year by an FAA inspector. Although this procedure puts quite a burden on the applicant taking the check ride, it does serve to keep the examiner on his toes.

Obviously this elaborate and comprehensive standardization program is a far cry from the days of "Bless you, go forth and give flight tests." If the examiner does his or her job, and most do, the thorough examination set forth in the Practical Test Standards makes it is extremely difficult for an unqualified applicant to slip through.

I have been told by the FAA, "If it bothers you to bust an applicant, you shouldn't be an examiner." Well, I have to tell you it has bothered me almost every single time I've had to turn one down. Believe me, I am abundantly aware of just how much time, effort, and emotional energy (not to mention money) the applicant has put into reaching this point. Of course it bothers me when one has to go away disappointed. But when an applicant really fails to meet the standard, I've done the person a favor by requiring that he or she go back to the instructor for some more dual or ground instruction prior to being turned loose in the airspace. Over the years, I've had several applicants come back some time later and tell me it was a good thing they had to take the test twice, because they didn't feel completely ready the first time.

Now, as a result of the adverse publicity brought on by a few extreme examples, the entire examiner program has been brought into question. In response to the *Wall Street Journal* article, the National Transportation Safety Board (NTSB) demanded that the FAA do something. Several proposals were immediately offered for improving the terrible situation described in the *Journal*. A few years ago, the manager of one Flight Standards District Office stated that he wanted fewer examiners giving more flight tests. Now it seems the policy is to have more examiners giving fewer flight tests. No examiner is to administer more than two check rides in a day. Any very active examiner who does a lot of flight testing (although "a lot" has not been defined) is to be watched closely to see that he or she is not being too easy on the applicants. However, one FAA District Office schedules each operations inspector for three flight tests per day.

The Aviation Consumer, quoting the NTSB recommendation, says, "Presumably, once applicants get word that a particular examiner is tough on flight tests, they look for one who's easier." This just isn't so. As I pointed out earlier, the most active examiner I know about in one district is also the one with the highest bust rate. The reason for his extreme activity is availability. He is noted for being able to schedule an applicant for a check ride with one or two days' notice. In the same district, it usually takes three weeks to get on the schedule of another examiner who has a reputation for practically giving away certificates and ratings. This latter examiner conducts about 30 check rides per year in comparison to the 300 for the tougher examiner. So much for the theory that there is a strong economic incentive for examiners to approve unqualified applicants to attract more business.

One of the NTSB's proposals would have the FAA assign applicants to designees on some kind of rotation basis. This would be absolutely unworkable because different designees have different degrees of availability—some are corporate pilots, some air carrier pilots, some charter pilots, some working flight instructors, and at least one is a staff member of a state aeronautics commission. All have other activities in addition to working as Designated Pilot Examiners. Then, too, they are scattered throughout the geographic areas of their respective districts, and such an assignment procedure would cause a considerable inconvenience on the applicant who would be required to travel to the other end of the district to meet the examiner who was next up for assignment.

Aviation Safety says in its "Bad Apple" examiner article "NTSB . . . would like to put more teeth in the FAA's ability to dismiss misfit DPEs. . . . The problem is that the procedures for 'de-designation' are complex. . . . The FAA's hands should be untied to give the heave-ho to examiners who knowingly approve pilots for flying privileges for which they are obviously unprepared." Well, just how complex does it have to be to tie the FAA's hands? When I was designated, I was told, "Remember, the FAA giveth and the FAA can taketh away!"

The Examiner's Manual, Order 8710.3A, which all examiners live by, says, in part:

31. CANCELLATION. A designation may be canceled by the designating field office on the basis of any of the following:

a. There is no longer a need for the examiner's services

b. Continued unsatisfactory performance in any phase of examiner duties or responsibilities. . . .

c. Any action(s) by the examiner which may reflect discredit on the FAA. . . .

d. Demonstrated inability of the examiner to work harmoniously with personnel of the district office or with the public. . . .

e. Confirmation of evidence that the examiner's general or professional qualifications and requirement were, in fact, not

*met at the time of the original designation, or are not met at
any time thereafter.*

*f. The inability of the examiner to demonstrate satisfactory
performance during a knowledge and skill evaluation (flight
test) or during a recurrent training . . . course.*

*g. The inability of an examiner to demonstrate qualifications
for any certificate or ratings held, or for which the examiner
holds a designation. . . .*

Does it sound as though it is complex or difficult to remove examiners who aren't doing their jobs?

One of the NTSB suggestions to the FAA has a great deal of merit,
and with the computer set-up at the Aeronautical Center in Oklahoma
City, it would not be particularly difficult to implement. The proposal
would have the FAA track the applicants passed into the system by
each examiner and correlate accidents, incidents, and violations with
the examiner who certified the pilot. As Mark Lacagnina put it in *Aviation Safety*, "Such a record would be helpful in spotting trends and
either setting straight or weeding out more of the 'bad apples'."

Any move to turn over all certification to the FAA itself would ne-
cessitate the hiring of several hundred more inspectors, and what's to
say that all inspectors possess all the sterling qualities demanded of
an examiner or inspector. In fact, there are no doubt a few "bad apple" inspectors who have slipped through the cracks in the system
and are out there doing less than an outstanding job.

While it is true that the failure rate for applicants tested by FAA inspectors is substantially higher than for Designated Examiners, it was
not always so. At least in part as a response to the outcry in the popular press and the pressure from the NTSB, the gap has widened drastically in recent years. Whereas in 1984 examiners failed 9.47% and
inspectors 10.8%, in 1988 the failure rate for examiners rose to 10% but
for inspectors it reached a whopping 32.5%! And when we look at original private pilot applications, we see 12.9% rejected by examiners and
59.3% by inspectors! Are our flight instructors so bad that only 40.7% of
their training product can meet the requirements of the private pilot
Practical Test Standards? I think not. Is it perhaps, as Mark Lacagnina
wrote,". . . . the possibility that FAA inspectors maintain a high failure
rate to discourage the extra workload they'd have to bear?"

On the whole, the vast majority of examiners are doing a conscientious job of applying the standards in each flight test they conduct,
just as most inspectors do. And although there are flight instructors
who shop for "easy" examiners to pass their applicants, most instructors want their students to get a comprehensive check ride, and most
applicants really want to be thoroughly tested.

B

The flight review

Although it is not a test in the strict sense of the word, in that it is not a pass-fail situation, the flight review is an evaluation of the pilot's knowledge and skill. Almost 25 years ago the FAA selected a General Aviation Operations Inspector in each of two District Offices (Detroit and Grand Rapids Districts in the Great Lakes Region), designated them Accident Prevention Specialists, and charged them with responsibility of establishing a program on a test basis. Each of these two inspectors selected several flight instructors in his district to work as volunteer Accident Prevention Counselors, and they began developing a workable safety program for pilots. At the end of the test year the concept proved worthwhile, and the accident prevention program was born. It went national, and one inspector in every district office was chosen to act as Accident Prevention Specialist.

One of the features of the original program was the "safety pin," lapel pin in the shape of a safety pin with the *Spirit of St. Louis* in the center. This pin was awarded to any pilot who took a "voluntary proficiency check ride" with one of the Accident Prevention Counselors. After a few successful years, the voluntary proficiency check became mandatory, and the biennial flight review (BFR) was born.

The powers that be at the very top of the Flight Standards section of the FAA believed and still believe that since professional pilots (particularly air carrier pilots) are required to get retraining and proficiency checks, why shouldn't the general-aviation pilot as well? The casual or infrequent flyer no doubt needs to have his or her skills (and knowledge) reviewed more than the professional who flies every day.

From its very inception, the BFR has been left entirely to the discretion of the administering instructor. This, of course, has resulted in the review consisting of anything from a perfunctory "once around the patch" to several dual instruction sessions involving several hours of flying. The FAA has carefully refrained from specifying specific maneuvers or procedures to be used in the conduct of the review. In other words, the FAA has imposed no requirements on the instructor, but it has offered suggestions in an effort to standardize the procedures as to just how the review might be conducted. In what seemed like no time at all, however, as soon as the review became regulatory, virtually every commercial publishing house in the business came out with a checklist of material covered on a BFR.

Of course, the definitive guide for the flight review is the FAA Advisory Circular, AC 61.98A. Although this description of recommended procedures for the conduct of a flight review is in text form, it is, in effect, a checklist that the instructor may use as a guide in the conduct of the review. One of the many FAA accident-prevention publications is a checklist to guide the instructor administering a review. The review itself is not meant to be a pass-fail situation, but without a "satisfactory" endorsement from the instructor (reviewer), the applicant (reviewee) may not legally operate as pilot-in-command of an aircraft (even solo). Therefore, despite protestations to the contrary, every pilot must "pass" the review.

Since the purpose of the review is to ensure that all pilots maintain the level of proficiency they reached at the time they acquired the certificate in the first place, the ideal review involves the use of our old friend the Practical Test Standards (PTS) as the guide for the conduct of the review. And the FAA is now pushing this as the guide for an instructor giving a review. If the pilot fails to meet the standard set forth in the appropriate PTS, the instructor should not issue him or her a "sat" on the review. Rather, the instructor should sign the reviewee's log showing that he or she received dual instruction for that session and then require another period (or more) until the pilot once again achieves the standard of the PTS prior to the instructor signing off on a flight review. Let the PTS be the guide. After all, that's what applied in the first place. Or did it? Perhaps the pilot acquired his or her certificate under an old, different standard, in which case maybe he or she should be "grandfathered" in under that standard. You can't very well ask pilots to be better than they were when they got the certificate.

Personally, when I administer a flight review, I hold the pilot to the standard of the appropriate PTS, but I select only those procedures and maneuvers that, in my judgment, are most beneficial for the pilot. I always include flight at minimum controllable airspeed while maneuvering the airplane and maintaining a precise altitude, a stall series (with emphasis on stall recognition as opposed to a mere demonstration of stalling the aircraft and recovering), and several landings, including crosswind, short and soft field, no flap landings, and slips. We usually also do one or more maximum performance takeoffs. Additionally, I give an oral test that includes, as a minimum, airspace regulations, fundamental aerodynamics, and weight and balance.

I spend a great deal of time providing expert testimony in legal actions involving airplane accidents, and in the vast majority of aircraft mishaps, weight and balance is a factor. It may not be the *determining* factor, but it is *a* factor, and often it is *the* cause of the accident. When it is, it's almost invariably fatal. In terms of fundamental aerodynamics, I cover the subjects of angle of attack and stalls, as well as maneuvering speed and how it affects safety.

If the pilot seeking a review holds a commercial certificate, I ask him or her to do a few of the commercial maneuvers (chandelles, lazy eights, and steep power turns), because the skill level in terms of maneuvering the airplane smoothly and precisely is what basically separates the commercial pilot from the private. By the bye, one can tell a great deal about the skill of a pilot by how well he or she does steep power turns of 360 or 720 degrees. The depth to which I go in the administration of a flight review depends on just how well I know the individual (as an *aviator*, not as a *person*). If he or she has been flying regularly and, to my knowledge, has been staying abreast of what's been happening in aviation, I don't give as comprehensive a review as I do for the infrequent flyer (or the individual with whose skills I am not familiar).

Even so, probably the most violated of all the Federal Aviation Regulations is Part 61.56 (formerly 61.57), which sets forth the requirements of the flight review. It seems to be easier for the pilot to forget the biennial flight review than the medical every 6, 12 , or 24 months, as the case may be. A large group of pilots have the infamous anti-authority attitude and maintain that they have nothing to prove and refuse to expose themselves to an instructor for a review of their skills and abilities. After all, they did it at the time they acquired the certificate, so why should they have to do it again? The irony of this is that these can be the pilots who need it most! The serious, safety-minded pilot who is very current and who conscientiously presents himself or herself to an instructor for a review every 24 months (or more often) is the one who benefits from the review the least.

The most recent changes in the evolution of the flight review regulations include the on-again, off-again, on-again annual flight review for the recreational or private pilot who has less than 400 hours total flight experience, or, in the case of the private pilot, does not have an instrument rating on his or her pilot certificate. Another change is the requirement of a minimum of one hour of ground and one hour of flight time on the review (annual or biennial). These refinements in the requirements of the flight review have been proposed, abandoned, and reproposed, and now, for the first time, the discretion of the administering flight instructor has been restricted by imposing a minimum time requirement. But this requirement is again under review by the regulators.

Another proposal for change in the review requirements (which, fortunately, has fallen by the wayside) called for the review to be accomplished in the most complex aircraft the pilot is qualified to fly. Then there was the proposal that every pilot be reviewed in every category and class of aircraft for which he or she is certificated. We are, however, still in the position of permitting a pilot who holds an ATP Certificate (with several type ratings) for Airplanes Single Engine Land and Rotorcraft-Helicopter, Commercial Privileges for Airplanes Multiengine Land and Single Engine Sea, and Private Privileges for Gliders and Lighter than Air Hot Air Balloon with Airborne Heater to take his or her flight review in a glider or a balloon, which covers the pilot in all the aircraft in which he or she is certificated.

There are several other ways of satisfactorily accomplishing the required flight review in addition to the pilot demonstrating to a Certified Flight Instructor that he or she can still meet the standard met when he or she received a certificate. The acquisition of a new grade of certificate or rating on a certificate counts as a flight review, but the applicant *must fly*. (For example, a CFI who renews his or her instructor certificate without actually flying with an examiner or inspector *still* requires a flight review, while the instructor who renews as a result of a flight test is covered as having been reviewed.) In fact, any *required* check ride counts as a flight review, and this is true whether it is a pass-fail situation or merely a standardization ride.

Another way to get credit for having completed a satisfactory review is to participate in the *WINGS* program. This program, now entering its 10th year, has enjoyed nothing less than phenomenal success. Any certificated pilot (above student grade) who attends an FAA Pilot Education (Safety) program, and within 365 days (formerly 60 days) of doing so receives three hours of dual instruction, including one hour of takeoffs and landings, one hour of air work (maneuvers, stalls, slow flight, etc.), and one hour of instrument instruction, is awarded a certificate attesting to his or her interest in safe flying and an attractive lapel pin (in the shape of a pair of wings—hence the name of the program). Once each year, the pilot may repeat the process (attend the safety seminar and get the three hours of instruction) and upgrade his or her *WINGS* from the present stage to the next stage up the ladder. The pin itself is derivative of military wings, from Pilot Wings (with a shield) through Senior Pilot (with a star above the shield) to Command Pilot (with a wreath around the star above the shield), and it makes quite an attractive lapel pin. Each stage (or, more properly, phase) of the *WINGS* program offers successively fancier wings pins for the lapel.

Human beings have a need to know that what they do makes a difference, that there is some means of measuring the results of their efforts, and for several years I felt a great sympathy for Accident Prevention Specialists, who could put forth a monumental amount of work and never *know* that they prevented a single accident. In our local FAA District Office, we have had nine Accident Prevention Specialists (or APS) over the years, plus several who acted as APS for one month only. (While we were between APSs, the office manager assigned each General Aviation Operations Inspector to fill the position for one month.) While I was sitting in the office of one APS, he kept reaching over and making a tally mark on his wall with a piece of chalk. I asked him what he was doing, and he said, "Look out the window there. Another airplane just landed, and I prevented another accident!"

The first actual measurement of success in this area came with the advent of the *WINGS* program. It is my understanding that after the first full year of this program, some 20,000 pilots had earned first-stage wings, and so far as we know, *not a single one of them had been involved in a reportable accident, incident, or violation.* This is an extremely impressive record and has made me a vigorous supporter of the program.

One thing that does not qualify as a flight review is an Instrument Competency Check (ICC), which, although required of the pilot who has permitted his instrument currency to lapse, is only a check of his ability to fly on the gauges and operate in the IFR system and is not a check of skill level as related to the *grade* of certificate the pilot holds. Therefore, an ICC cannot be offered in place of a BFR. They are two entirely different kinds of checks. The two may be combined in a single transaction, and they frequently are.

In considering a flight review, perhaps pilots, and particularly flight instructors, might ask, "Just how good should a pilot be?" Once again, the PTS comes into play. The answer, of course, is "At least good enough to meet the minimum standard as set forth in the Practical Test Standards for his or her grade of certificate, a standard met at the time the pilot was originally tested."

C

How good
is pilot testing?

If the objective of pilot certification is to ensure that only safe, accident-free, and violation-free pilots find their way into the airspace, we have a basis of measuring just how well we are doing throughout the current certification process. And the certification process is certainly not static. It is constantly evolving.

The pilot applicant must demonstrate to the satisfaction of the Administrator of the Federal Aviation Administration (FAA) that he or she has the requisite aeronautical knowledge (primarily demonstrated by a written examination with a cut-off score of 70), aeronautical skill (demonstrated to an FAA inspector or Designated Pilot Examiner on the practical test, which is a pass-fail criterion-based examination), and aeronautical experience (acquired by training with a Certified Flight Instructor and solo practice) to be entrusted with the privileges of each of the certificates and ratings offered by the FAA. Each of these gates through which the applicant must pass on the way to certification stands alone, but all the requirements must be met for certification.

The test results can be measured against the accident and violation record of the individual pilot. It also can be determined what, if any, correlation exists between success on the knowledge level and the skill level and the skill level and the experience level. Knowledge and experience are measured empirically, but skill is judged on a pass-fail basis.

Keep in mind that the cut-off score for the written test (designed to evaluate knowledge only) is 70 percent, while the cut-off score for the practical examination (testing for the skill requirement on the flight portion and the knowledge requirement on the oral portion) is 100 percent, since *all* TASKS must be satisfactorily demonstrated. Please note that testing for the knowledge requirement continues right through the practical test as well as the written. In other words, this requirement might not be completely satisfied by the written examination.

To determine if a positive correlation exists between knowledge and experience, we need only compare the applicant's score against hours of experience. Do those with high scores on the written tend to have more experience? We can also compare knowledge and experience against success on the practical test. Are those who do well on the written also more likely to pass the practical than those who don't do well on the written? Are those with more hours of experience more likely to pass the practical than those with less?

What effect does experience have on the likelihood of the pilot being involved in a mishap or a violation? With respect to mishaps (accidents or incidents), we can answer the question, but at the present time we don't have a way to make that determination with respect to violations. The statistics are not currently available, but in future years, with a recently introduced tracking system (inaugurated in 1992), we will be able to track violations as well. The FAA now has a system in place by which a pilot's record can be backtracked through the examiner or inspector who issued the certificate or rating all the way to the recommending instructor. The ever-present Big Brother is now able to not only check the record of every pilot who holds a certificate, but also tell who certified and who recommended the pilot for each certificate and rating held. Scary, isn't it?

There seems to be no relationship whatsoever between an individual's score on the written examination and his or her ability to pass the practical test. An applicant who scores 100 is no more likely to pass than one who scores 70. In this case, the old saw that holds that "70 is as good as 100" seems to be accurate. If the written does indeed test for the knowledge requirement, and the practical for the skill requirement, then there is apparently no relationship between an individual's knowledge and skill as an aviator. Personally, I find this hard to believe. I believe if there is no relationship between knowledge and skill, then there's something wrong with one or the other means of testing. To me, it seems that if an applicant knows and understands the purpose and mechanics of a procedure or maneuver, he or she should be able to perform it, at least within the minimal tolerance of the test requirements. Of course, most of the material for which the written examination tests bears no relationship to the manipulation of the aircraft through the required maneuvers.

On the other hand, it has been demonstrated by a group of more than 500 ground school students that those who have at least *some* flight training (hands-on experience) score between 6 and 10 points more on average than those who complete the ground school entirely in an academic setting without any flight experience prior to taking the written examination. In other words, academic study is rendered more meaningful if the student has at least a smattering of experience in the airplane itself. This principle has been proven time and again. But flight experience seems to bear little relationship to academic work.

Also there does seem to be a substantial correlation between experience and success on the practical test on which performance is measured against a set of clearly defined objectives. The applicant who exceeds the minimum experience requirement by a large margin is more likely to pass the practical than the one who barely meets the minimum. Skill is enhanced by practice and experience. Since greater experience has been proven to result in greater success on the skill portion of the certification requirement, shouldn't the minimum experience requirement be raised? This idea has been kicking around for years, and each time it has come up in the form of a proposal, it has bumped up against the economic reality of the cost of training and gaining experience. Even so, the last major change in the FAA requirements for the certification of commercial pilots saw a substantial increase in the amount of time necessary to meet the experience requirement (from 200 to 250 hours under FAR Part 61, the basic certification regulation). Formerly, the commercial certificate was a sort of glorified private, but with the increasing sophistication of the equipment flown today, anyone who is to be entrusted with the responsibility of carrying passengers or property for hire should have more experience (and have some of it in fairly complex equipment) than what was previously required. Today, commercial applicants are not only tested to a higher standard of smoothness and precision in the manipulation of the controls, but they are required to demonstrate knowledge of and skill in the operation of more sophisticated equipment.

There is a substantial positive relationship between experience and mishaps. The greater the experience level of the pilot, the less likely he or she is to be involved in an accident, despite the fact that more experience translates to more exposure. Accident statistics have demonstrated that this is especially true of the complex single-engine airplane and the light twin. The relatively inexperienced pilot is more likely to bend this kind of airplane than is the high-timer. A positive step to correct this problem is the fairly recent requirement for an instructor endorsement for the high-performance single. There is, however, still no minimum experience requirement for the addition of a multiengine class rating to a pilot certificate. All the applicant has to do is meet the published standard of knowledge and skill on a practical test.

Apparently pilot experience does not help in the matter of violations, for the high-time pilot seems to be just as likely to commit a violation as the beginner. This is even true of air carrier pilots, who have a much better accident record than general aviation pilots but are no better off in the case of violations. One would think that air carrier pilots, who not only have to live by the FAA regulations but the regulations of the companies for which they fly, which are invariably more stringent than those of the FAA, would be less prone to be involved in violations of the FARs, but such is not the case.

In his outstanding doctoral dissertation titled *Criterion Referenced Measurement: A Bayesian Validation of the Beta-binomial Prediction Model*, Joseph F. Kearney made the following major recommendations for change in the certification process:

1 Require training and testing on decision-making.
2 Require knowledge of inappropriate behavior and behavior modification.
3 Raise the 70 percent cut-off score on the written test.

He believes these recommendations will improve the certification process. He does stop short, however, of recommending an increase in the experience requirement, a recommendation one might expect since it is in this area that the most dramatic results might be expected. As mentioned previously, over the years the FAA has repeatedly looked at the possibility of increasing the experience requirement for the private certificate. In fact, a step backwards might be said to have been taken with the introduction of the Recreational Pilot Certificate, which requires less experience than the basic private. This new grade of certificate was introduced as an entry-level certification with, hopefully, a reduced investment on the part of the applicant. It was further hoped that the holder of a Recreational Pilot Certificate would be inspired to go forward with his or her training and achieve Private Pilot status.

No doubt these changes would result in releasing better-qualified airmen (and women) into the system. However, the procedure for implementing and administering these changes would be extremely difficult, if not impossible. During the certification flight test, pilot examiners are supposed to ensure that each applicant has reviewed and corrected any and all mistakes he or she made on the written test. While this procedure might not be as good a means of ensuring that the applicant's knowledge is up to snuff as raising the requirement for passing the written to 80, 90, or 100 percent, it is probably an adequate compromise. If the examiners do their job properly and quiz all applicants on all areas missed on the written, then requiring a higher score on the written would accomplish little, if anything.

The FAA is already addressing, in part, the first of Dr. Kearney's suggestions with the current emphasis on CRM (cockpit resource management). Multi-pilot crews are being trained to make joint decisions based on the best available information, and single-pilot crews are being better trained in the use of checklists and individual decision-making. Even so, the entire area of training for decision-making could stand more attention.

With respect to the second of Dr. Kearney's recommendations, the FAA is just now beginning to recognize the need for training and knowledge of inappropriate behavior and behavior modification. Although this is not strictly in the area of medical factors, the FAA has recently begun to place emphasis on the pilot's knowledge of the effects of medical factors on flight. Attention is now being given to the pilot's state of mind and emotional health.

Of course, Dr. Kearney's recommendations aren't the only ones to be put forth for improving the certification process. There's always the continuing controversy regarding the possible reintroduction of spin training in the primary curriculum. The most recent compromise in this area is the requirement for a discussion of spins during the pilot's training. Perhaps reading and talking about spins is enough without the requirement of actually demonstrating spins. Only the passage of time can answer this one.

Contrary to the situation that prevailed just a few years ago, today there is an ongoing program of standardization of pilot examiners. A small group of dedicated teachers, under the leadership of Ron Bragg, has put together a program of indoctrination for new examiners in an attempt to standardize the testing process. The program is updated every two years. Attendance at this program biannually is compulsory on the part of all examiners, and a passing grade on the final examination given at the conclusion of each program is required for the examiner to retain his or her designation.

All in all, the present system of testing and certification of pilots seems to be working quite well. The accident rate has been steadily falling in recent years, but no one will be satisfied until it reaches zero and stays there. This goal might not be attainable, but we must keep striving to reach it.

D

The 10 most common reasons for failing flight tests

The only real reason applicants fail to pass check rides is lack of preparation. That said, we can look at some of the more common ways in which lack of preparation shows up.

The examiner must justify the issuance of a Disapproval Notice by entering a reason related to one or more of the required "Pilot Operations" spelled out in FAR Part 61. This justification on the part of the examiner comes in the form of entering on the Notice of Disapproval (pink slip) which Task (or Tasks) in which Area or Areas in which Pilot Operation or Operations the applicant failed. Remember, the "Pilot Operations" are regulatory, and the examiner had better nail down any failure to a specific Pilot Operation or he or she is leaving himself or herself open to a challenge by the failed applicant!

The examiner has no authority to impose his or her own limits on the applicant's performance. Rather, the examiner must strictly adhere to the limits set forth in the Practical Test Standards for whatever certificate or rating the applicant is seeking. The examiner can't go by what the applicant or the recommending instructor knows the applicant can do, only by what the applicant shows the examiner at the time of the flight test, even if the examiner has seen the applicant perform the task flawlessly on a previous occasion.

In the most recent three and a half years I have administered 1,116 flight tests and have had to disapprove 166 applications. This comes out to a bust rate of 14.87%, just about the nationwide average for Designated Pilot Examiners. The total Tasks failed is much greater than the number of individual applicants failing, because many applicants failed more than one Task on a single bust. In determining the 10 most common Tasks failed, I lumped private and commercial check rides together, and I separated Instrument Rating applications but have included Multiengine Class Rating applicants who failed the instrument portion of the multiengine check ride with the instrument list. I did not work up a list of multiengine failures other than those who failed the instrument portion of the multiengine flight test, and who, as stated, are included with the instrument rating applicants. Of 126 failures on private pilot flight tests, 43 failed on the oral without ever getting to the airplane! This is an amazing 34% of the total. Of those who failed the oral, 37, or 86%, lacked basic knowledge of the airspace regulations. The other six, or 14%, of the oral busts were on cross-country planning. Two of those applicants spent more than two hours on their flight planning, exclusive of the time they were talking to Flight Service on the telephone. The regulations allow a half hour. I don't know a single examiner who demands that it be done in the allotted half hour, but more than two hours is a bit much! If they take 45 minutes to an hour, it's not too bad, but much over that just cannot be allowed.

The number one cause for failure on private and commercial tests is, therefore, lack of knowledge of the regulations. On the private test, this takes the form of failure on airspace regs, but on the commercial test, it is usually a lack of knowledge of the privileges and limitations of the commercial certificate. To avoid violating the regulations, we must know what they are—ignorance is no excuse!

The next most frequent Task failures involved the stall series. A total of 27 applicants failed in this area, almost all of whom were private applicants, and the vast majority of them failed to clear the area prior to attempting the stall maneuvers. Virtually all could make a stall and recover, but stall recognition is another matter entirely. Even more fundamental is the necessity of looking around thoroughly to make sure the area is clear of any possible traffic, and I am absolutely dumbfounded by the number of test applicants who, when asked for an imminent stall, simply yank back on the yoke, stand the airplane on its tail until a violent break occurs, point the nose at the ground, and cram on the power, all without making any attempt to clear the area—no clearing turns and not even a good look outside the cockpit!

The next most frequent cause for failure on the private check ride was on the instrument tasks. In this area there were 11 failures, or 9%

of the total. A few were unable to keep the airplane upright while maneuvering (climbing, descending, or turning), but most failed on recovery from unusual attitudes—usually a "graveyard spiral."

Tied for fourth and fifth as the most popular ways to bust a flight test were the tasks associated with emergency procedures and cross-country flying. In these two areas there were 9 failures each (7% of the total). When confronted with the loss of the only engine, some applicants spent time frantically attempting a restart without ever achieving the best glide speed or locating a suitable landing area; some got so far off course on their cross-country flying that they became hopelessly lost; others were unable to locate and fly to an alternate when diverted. (Along the way to the destination on the cross-country portion of the flight test, the examiner can announce that the weather is closing in and we must fly to the nearest airport and land.)

The sixth most popular bust is crosswind takeoffs. Seven, or 5.5% of the total, of the failures were on this task—not a lot, but a significant factor in the accident picture when we look at the number of airplanes that get bent as a result of poor crosswind-landing technique.

In seventh place is faulty cross-country planning, explained previously in the discussion of failures on the oral part of the test. Six applicants, or 3.6%, failed for this reason.

In eighth place, five applicants busted the check ride because of an inability to track a VOR. Most examiners fail the nav radios of those applicants who plan their cross-country trip exclusively by the use of the VOR and require that the applicant demonstrate that he or she knows how to navigate by pilotage. Conversely, if all the planning was done by pilotage and/or ded reckoning (short for "deduced reckoning"), the examiner will make the applicant demonstrate the ability to use the VOR. Both are required tasks. These five failures comprise 3% of all my busts.

Four distinct tasks with three failures tied for ninth place on the list. I'll treat each of these four separately.

Back on the oral phase, three applicants were unable to compute a weight-and-balance problem. Some applicants attempt to use the hypothetical weight and center of gravity for the airplane in the sample found in the airplane handbook, and when they are told they must use the actual data from the airplane we will be flying, some don't know where to find this information. Even given the opportunity to get it together, three applicants were unable to work out our location in the envelope, locate the CG, or tell whether or not we were within the gross weight of the airplane. I might sound like a nut on the subject of weight and balance, but I spend a lot of time on a witness stand in a court of law providing expert testimony on aviation accident cases, and in almost every light-plane accident report I've ever studied (and I've studied a lot of them), weight and balance is a factor. Ofttimes it is the cause of the accident, and when it is, it is usually fatal!

The soft-field landing task also racked up three failures. Some students seeking the private certificate seem to be unable to successfully make a soft (or a short) field landing. The primary reason is a lack of ability to accurately control airspeed. The approach is too fast, the airplane gets somewhere near the ground, the applicant yanks back on the yoke, and the airplane zooms up a few feet, quits flying, and goes "thunk."

Another three private applicants failed to set the heading indicator, directional gyro, gyroscopic compass, or whatever we are calling it this week, prior to takeoff. This oversight threw off their cross-country flying, and these three might also be reflected among the nine who busted on cross-country flying. Many pilots set the heading indicator during the engine run-up, while they are changing power settings and before the gyro has fully erected. If they're smart, they will check it again with the runway heading when they are on the takeoff roll.

Three more failed on entry to the traffic pattern at an uncontrolled (no tower) airport. As might be expected, those applicants trained at a busy, controlled airport (I work at the 22nd busiest airport in the United States) seem to have trouble entering the pattern and landing at a quiet field. Some 20 miles or so from our home field is an airport with a single paved strip, and I frequently divert my applicants to this airport on the cross-country task. The main runway at our home airport is 300 feet wide and more than 6,000 feet long, and the airport to which I sometimes divert the applicants is only 24 feet wide and 2,600 feet long. From pattern altitude it looks like a sidewalk, and those used to the big one back home just can't seem to get the picture. I sometimes do something even worse, diverting the applicant to another nearby airport with a 100-foot by 2,500-foot turf runway, at which time I am occasionally told, "I can't land there—there's no pavement!" On the other side of the coin; I frequently get applicants trained at uncontrolled (nontower) airports who have a problem with radio communication.

Finally, in 10th place are two applicants who banged the tail on the soft-field takeoff task. In an "Eye of the Examiner" column, I covered the subject of the inability of many applicants to perform two tasks simultaneously. If there any crosswind component and I call for a soft-field takeoff, the applicant frequently concentrates so intently on keeping the nose up out of the hypothetical mud or slush that he or she forgets all about the crosswind, and we lift off gently drifting off the runway heading.

While these are the 10 most common reasons for failure on the private check ride, two fairly common problem tasks on the commercial ride are the steep power turn (during which the applicant fails to hold altitude within tolerance, and during which on one occasion the applicant rolled out 90 degrees off his heading) and the descending three-turn spiral, during which the applicant sometimes lets airspeed get away from him or her.

The top three causes of failure on the instrument check ride (including multiengine applicants seeking instrument privileges) follow:

1 Instrument approaches. A total of 35 applicants busted their flight tests for failure to properly execute one or another of the required approaches. Either they busted minimums (or neglected to descend from the final fix and went sailing right over the airport several hundred feet high) or they exceeded the lateral limits.

2 Two areas are tied at eight busts each. One is lack of knowledge of regulations (here we go again); the other is failure to comply with ATC clearances. Once again, how can we avoid violating the regulations if we don't know what they are? And anytime we deviate from a clearance we are leaving ourselves open to a violation, a situation to be avoided if at all possible!

3 The only other instrument failures that occurred more than once for the same reason were the three who busted for failure to hold altitude.

Most of the examiners in my district average about 30 flight tests a year, so I didn't poll them, because their input would not be significant. However, one other examiner does about as many as I do. He is a retired FAA inspector and a good friend of mine. His bust rate is about the same as mine, and when I asked him to list the 10 most common reasons for failure on check rides, he unhesitatingly informed me that there's only one reason an applicant ever fails, and that's lack of preparation.

When pressed to list specifics, he said that most failures on the oral were because of lack of knowledge of the airspace regulations, and on the flight portion of the practical test, it was stalls. Are you surprised? Following these were landings, particularly slips to a landing, and steep turns. An informal survey of several other examiners (no hard numbers) came up with substantially the same results, so the areas that instructors need to work on to better prepare their applicants to pass their check rides are pretty clear.

Here's a summary of the results of my survey:

Private and Commercial Applicants

Rank	Reason	Number of applicants	Percent of busts
1	Lacks knowledge of airspace regulations	37	29%
2	Stalls	27	21%
3	Flight by reference to instruments	11	9%
4	Emergency procedures	9	7%
5	Cross-country flying	9	7%
6	Crosswind takeoffs	7	6%
7	Cross-country planning	6	5%
8	VOR tracking	5	4%
9	Soft-field landing	3	2%
	Weight and balance	3	2%
	Failure to set heading indicator	3	2%
	Traffic pattern	3	2%
10	Soft-field takeoff	2	2%

Instrument Applicants

Rank	Reason	Number of applicants	Percent of busts
1	Approaches	35	54%
2	Compliance with ATC clearance	8	12%
3	Knowledge of regulations	8	12%
4	Holding altitude	2	3%

E

The
violation
alternative

Although what follows has very little to do with flight testing, unless it comes under Regulation 609, it is so important that every active pilot should be thoroughly familiar with this material. Read it carefully.

Lord knows I don't always agree with everything the feds do, but the Remedial Training Program is a program that I wholeheartedly endorse. As far as I can determine, the only negative factor in the Remedial Training Program is that it is not being used to the extent that it should be. Here is that rare concept—a win-win situation, and in large measure, it is being ignored.

Everybody involved in the Remedial Training Program comes out ahead. The pilot is certainly fortunate in that he or she not only doesn't suffer a suspension of certificate, but after two years, the incident is expunged from his or her record. The investigating FAA Aviation Safety Inspector wins, unless he or she is one of those rare individuals who enjoys paperwork, because once the program is offered and accepted, the inspector is out of it entirely, reducing his or her workload. The office of the Regional Counsel is a winner since the remedial training alternative leaves it totally uninvolved, and this even reduces the workload of the drastically overworked Administrative Law Judges who work for the National Transportation Safety Board. The only person who has to work in this situation is the Safety Program Manager (SPM), formerly Accident Prevention Program Manager (APPM) and Accident Prevention Specialist (APS). Of course, that's his or her job anyway. A flight instructor also gets to work teaching the program laid out by the SPM, but again, that's what instructors get paid for doing.

On May 18, 1990, the FAA Administrator approved Compliance and Enforcement Bulletin 90-8, Corrective Action Through Remedial Training, and it became effective on that date. By June 12, 1990, just over three weeks later, the Associate Administrator for Regulation and Certification, in concert with the Chief Counsel, put out a memorandum to all Regional Flight Standards Division Managers and Regional Assistant Chief Counsels explaining and clarifying the Bulletin. The purpose of the memo was to prevent the FAA from making procedural mistakes that would permit a violator to escape unpunished. On October 11, 1990, Notice N 8700.4 was published by the then-Acting Director of the Flight Standards Service, Thomas Accardi, for incorporation into Orders 8700.1 and 8300.10, the General Aviation Operations Inspector's Handbook and the Airworthiness Inspectors Handbook, respectively.

Bulletin 90-8 spells out just who is eligible for remedial training and how the program is supposed to work. To begin with, only those airmen (pilot or mechanic) who inadvertently commit a violation and are not engaged in commercial activity at the time of the alleged violation are eligible. Some other factors can disqualify one from participation in the program, but a negative attitude, a deliberate violation, and a violation committed while engaged in commercial activity are the primary prohibiting factors. A history of previous violation weighs heavily in the determination as to whether or not remedial training will be offered, but even that is not absolutely prohibitive. Although intended primarily for first offenders, in some cases remedial training may be offered a repeat offender if all other factors indicate that he or she is a suitable candidate.

Prior to Bulletin 90-8, when a violation was brought to the attention of Flight Standards, the matter was assigned to an Aviation Safety Inspector, either Operations or Airworthiness, as the situation warranted. When, during the course of the investigation conducted by the assigned inspector, the name of the suspected violator came up, a letter was sent over the investigating inspector's signature. This letter, officially called the Letter of Investigation, or LOI, offered the alleged offender an opportunity to tell his or her side of the story, and it allowed 10 days to do so. *There was no legal requirement that this letter even be answered or otherwise acknowledged!* Even so, the receipt of a LOI is a frightening experience, and many airmen felt compelled by the wording of the letter to spill their guts and start spewing forth everything they knew or think they knew about the situation. Whatever they said not only could but most certainly would be used against them in whatever future action followed. In other words, the LOI was an invitation for the airman to incriminate himself, and it very often worked in just that fashion. In this situation, there is no constitutional protection against self-incrimination.

Compliance/Enforcement Bulletin 90-8 mandated, among other things, that the LOI *must* include mention of the possibility of remedial training, where appropriate. Without committing the FAA to a firm offer, the LOI is now supposed to include mention of remedial training as an alternative to sanction. The bulletin, in an appendix, even includes a model LOI containing this statement: "Additionally, you may be allowed to participate in the FAA's corrective action through remedial training program, in the place of legal enforcement action that may otherwise be deemed to be appropriate." It then goes on to spell out the requirements for eligibility in the program. Research indicates that this procedure, mandated by the Administrator, is not being followed in some district offices (FSDOs), at least by some inspectors. In fact, it is being widely ignored! Many letters go out to eligible alleged violators on an old form that makes no mention of remedial training as a method of resolving the situation.

Prior to Bulletin 90-8, after the LOI came, if the accused violator wished, he or she could have an informal conference with an Associate Regional Counsel. At this point, unless the airman could prove that at the time of the violation he or she was in jail, the hospital, China, or some such alibi that made it impossible that he or she committed the act, a sanction was imposed. The appeal is to an NTSB Administrative Law Judge, and from the judge's decision to the full Board.

However, if the violator is offered remedial training in the original LOI and chooses to accept the offer, the entire process stops and the situation is turned over to the Safety Program Manager (SPM) at the FSDO. The SPM's first step, after reviewing the investigating inspector's file on the case, is to sit down with the violator and discuss the situation. This personal, face-to-face meeting is mandatory. At this time, assuming a positive attitude on the part of the violator, a formal Training Agreement is signed by both the SPM and the violator. This agreement serves several purposes. Primarily it ensures that there shall be no misunderstanding regarding the terms and conditions under which the remedial training is to be undertaken. It also protects the FAA in the event the violator fails to live up to the terms of the agreement and complete the training within the proscribed time. If this should happen, the existence of the signed agreement prohibits the use of the "stale complaint" defense if the FAA should bring formal charges.

However, by far the most important part of the Training Agreement is the formal Remedial Training Syllabus it contains. This syllabus, designed by the SPM for the specific situation, contains the duration and nature of the ground and flight instruction required of the trainee, and it is tailored to provide the maximum training benefit based on the nature of the incident that violated one or more of the regulations. A sample (model) Training Agreement is included as an appendix to Bulletin 90-8. Once the Training Agreement is signed, all that remains is for a good, competent flight instructor to administer the training, and the instructor, trainee, and Safety Program Manager to follow through and see that all the bases are covered.

Case history

To see precisely how the program works, let's take an actual case and follow it through from its inception to its conclusion. It all started when a message was received at an FSDO in the Southern Region from an approach control facility advising that a pilot in a Cessna 172 had been "FLYING VFR WHEN IFR REQD . . . PILOT UNQUALIFIED FOR CONDITIONS . . . (airport manager) . . . CALLED AND ADVISED THAT N_____ HAD DEPARTED AND COULD NOT RELOCATE THE AIRPORT FOR LANDING . . . . PILOT CALLED ON FREQ____ AND ADVISED THAT HE WAS IN THE CLOUDS AND NOT IFR QUALIFIED . . . ." ATC then vectored the aircraft to an airport where VFR conditions existed and a safe landing was made.

The file was turned over to a General Aviation Operations Inspector at the local FSDO, and he placed a call to the pilot and left a message to contact him regarding a deviation that had occurred four days earlier. The following day the pilot returned the inspector's call, and the inspector wrote down his impressions of the telephone conversation so as to have a record for the file. The violator was asked to explain in his own words just what happened. He stated that he and his wife had planned a trip, had gone to the (uncontrolled) airport in the morning, and had loaded the airplane in anticipation of an afternoon departure. By the planned departure time, the weather had deteriorated to the extent that the planned flight was canceled. He and his wife returned to the airport and unloaded the airplane in preparation for making the trip by automobile. Before doing so, however, the pilot decided to make one circuit of the pattern in the airplane. He stated that he knew the visibility was low, but he believed the clouds were high enough for pattern operations, so he and his wife took off. Almost as soon as they were airborne, the pilot lost ground contact in fog and lost sight of the airport. He called a nearby approach control facility and received vectors for a climb to VFR conditions on top and then to an uncontrolled airport where a landing was made in VFR.

The inspector's written report of the telephone conversation goes on:

I asked how many persons were on board the aircraft. He stated he and his wife. I asked what the weather was prior to his departure. He said it was a little foggy, maybe one and one half to two miles; the clouds didn't appear to be below pattern altitude. I asked if he had received a weather briefing prior to the flight. He said he hadn't because he didn't plan on leaving the pattern. . . . I asked him for information concerning flight time and flight review date for the 8020-18 Investigation of Pilot Deviation Report. . . .

He asked what he could expect from the incident. I explained he would receive a (LOI), and it would be specific concerning procedures. He asked what the minimum penalty might be. I explained all the possible recommendations, from letter of warning to certificate action, including the possibility of remedial training. . . . [He] exhibited a very open and truthful attitude. He was remorseful and has apparently learned much from the incident.

Thereafter, the inspector completed the FAA Form 8020-18 Investigation of Pilot Deviation Report, including the statement, "Pilot attitude and concerns have been positive and constructive. [Pilot] would most likely benefit from remedial training. Remedial training is being considered pending completion of investigation."

The next step was the posting (Certified-Return Receipt Requested) of the LOI, which followed the recommended model, including mention of the possibility of participation in the remedial training program, and setting forth the conditions of eligibility for such participation. In this instance, the pilot met all the requirements, but he was not so informed in the LOI.

A week later the inspector received a reply from the pilot who was involved in the incident. It said, in part:

. . . Although the outcome was a good one, I put a lot of people to their test on that afternoon. I realize that for a five-minute go around the pattern, I endangered the life of my wife as well as my own life. Had it not been for the excellent job of the controllers. . . . I realize that this matter may be under investigation and I am willing to work with you and the FAA in any

way I possibly can to resolve this matter. I understand that I
have an option of working with you by taking Remedial
Training, if allowed, and I will receive no disciplinary action
against my pilot's license. Please allow me to go to and partic-
ipate in the Remedial Training Classes. . . .

The letter goes on to offer assurances that such an event will
never happen again and to again express his appreciation for the professionalism of the ATC personnel who rendered assistance and again
ask for remedial training in lieu of certificate action.

The next step was a letter over the signature of the Safety Program
Manager (SPM) at the Flight Standards District Office (FSDO) to the violator advising him that he was indeed eligible for participation in the
FAA remedial training program in lieu of legal enforcement action. En-
closed with this letter was a Remedial Training Syllabus and Agreement.
The violator had already nominated an instructor with whom he wished
to train, and the letter confirmed the approval of his nomination. The
letter further stated that the agreement must be signed during a personal visit between the violator and the SPM, that periodic progress reports must be made to the SPM, that the completion standards of all
elements of the training syllabus must be met within 30 days of the
signing of the agreement, that written documentation of this completion
must be provided (in the form of the instructor's signature on the original copy of the syllabus), and finally, that "all expenses incurred for the
prescribed training will be borne by you." The letter ends with the statement, "The administrative action will remain in your file for a two-year
period, after which time it will be deleted from your record."

The "Remedial Training Syllabus and Agreement" that accompa-
nied the letter from the SPM was the real meat of the program. It is
the syllabus that guides the instructor and the student (violator)
through the training, and the training is specifically designed by the
SPM for the maximum benefit based on the situation that triggered
the violation in the first place. For example, the syllabus and agreement prepared for the case discussed here called for five hours of
ground instruction on those sections of the *Airman's Information
Manual* (now *Aeronautical Information Manual*) dealing with meteorology and pilot/controller roles and responsibilities, several sections of the Aviation Weather book, those parts of the Federal
Aviation Regulations dealing with instrument rating equipment and
requirements, and instrument and visual flight rules. It also required
that a visit be made to "an Air Route Traffic Control Center or Radar
Approach Control Facility for a brief on IFR operations within the National Airspace System." This visit was to be attested to by the signature of the chief of the facility or by a duty supervisor.

Additionally, the syllabus and agreement mandated three hours of flight instruction, including "a VFR cross-country flight involving flight planning and the procurement of weather information . . . flight solely by reference to instruments . . . (and) . . . operations to/from an airport inside a Terminal Control Area." Both the flight and ground instruction were to be administered by a flight and/or ground instructor selected by the trainee and approved by the FSDO.

The syllabus also spelled out the completion standards for the training as follows: "The training will have been successfully completed when, by oral testing and practical demonstration, the airman demonstrates to the supervising instructor proficiency in the above (selected) subjects and procedures in accordance with the Private Pilot Practical Test Standards." The syllabus portion of the agreement was signed and dated by the SPM.

The agreement portion, including notice of the required completion date, was signed and dated by the trainee, and finally, a completion statement was included for the signature of the instructor, who signed and dated it for the trainee to return to the SPM at the FSDO. And when this was accomplished, the trainee needed only behave himself for two years, at which time the record would be cleared.

In interviewing both the instructor and the trainee involved in this case, I found both to be enthusiastic about the program. A very interesting and positive point emphasized several times by the trainee was how this experience had changed his attitude toward the FAA from one of fear and apprehension to that of friendly cooperation. This particular trainee acknowledged that he needed the training and affirmed that this experience led him to resolve to go on and undertake instruction for adding the instrument rating to his pilot certificate.

Success or failure?

Now that I have followed a single example of just how the remedial training alternative to certificate action type sanctions was accomplished, let's examine the program and see what is happening with it on the national scene.

On April 18, 1991, the Operations Branch General Aviation and Commercial Division issued a "Report Card" with a grade of A+ entitled "Remedial Training Program Evaluation Report."

Since it was determined that merely compiling the total letters of correction and relating them to specific Federal Aviation Regulations would not provide the desired detailed analysis, a questionnaire was constructed and mailed to 300 program participants. A phenomenal response to this voluntary questionnaire occurred—151 replies were received!

The 345 letters of correction received by the Operations Branch contained citations of 422 regulations violated. Not surprisingly, Part 91 of the regs, General Operating and Flight Rules, was violated most often (388 times), distantly followed by FAR Part 61, Certification: Pilots and Flight Instructors (15 citations). The remaining 19 rule violations were scattered among other FARs. The overwhelming majority of violations corrected by remedial training have been those dealing with the inadvertent penetration of controlled airspace of one sort or another. Altogether, there were 290 such incidents out of the 422 total in the sample, 69% of the total violations and 75% of the FAR Part 91 violations. Quite obviously this type of inadvertent violation lends itself very well to the remedial training program.

Of the slightly more than 50% return on the questionnaires sent out (151 out of 300), most (81%) asserted that the curriculum developed by the SPM was appropriate for their specific situation. A substantial majority of the respondents indicated a clear understanding of the curriculum objectives as well as understanding exactly what was expected of them in the training. Virtually all of the respondents indicated that they benefited from the training. If the violation occurred other than in the airman's home district, coordination was required between the investigating inspector where the event took place and the SPM in the local office convenient to the airman, and in those cases, the respondents indicated that it was well handled. The respondents were invited to comment on the program and were guaranteed anonymity, and most of them added comments to their responses to the survey questionnaire; these comments were universally favorable.

This report-card evaluation of the program near the end of its first year ended with the following conclusions and recommendations:

> *The Remedial Training Program has been well-received by the aviation public and has been highly effective both in returning safer airmen to the system and in assuring continued, future compliance with the FAR. The results of the participant survey validate the program and should be construed as an indication of the need for its continuance. . . . Because so many violations involved incursions into controlled airspace, FAA needs to ensure that pilot and instructor training and certification are adequate in this area.*

In view of this overwhelming indication of early success, one must ask why it was necessary for the Director of Flight Standards to issue a memo on June 13, 1994, pointing out that in the first three years there were an average of 550 remedial training cases per year, but in the fourth year there was a drop to 399 cases, and in the first half of the fifth year, there were only 20 cases (and 10 of them were in a single district office). This memo concludes, "All FSDO managers should reeducate their inspector work force on the program's policy and procedures. . . ."

Obviously something is missing. Perhaps established bureaucrats are prone to resist change and insist on doing things the same old way, or perhaps many Flight Standards Inspectors have the mindset that wants nothing to do with a kinder, gentler approach to enforcement, but for whatever reason the full potential of the Remedial Training Program is not being approached. Airmen should know that they have an absolute right to be informed regarding the program. Understand, they have no right to participate in the program, but they do have the right to be told about it in the original LOI, and even this isn't being done in many instances. If more airmen were aware of this alternative to punitive action, and more inspectors were reminded of their duty to try to use it, we would no doubt see a resurgence in its utilization. If the FAA wants to change its image from adversarial to cooperative, if it really wants their customers (the airmen) to believe it when they hear, "Hi, I'm from the FAA and I'm here to help you," then better use of the Remedial Training Alternative to help ensure compliance is one means of achieving this end. If this program becomes more widely utilized, replacing certificate action and/or civil penalty sanctions, everyone involved would benefit.

Index

About the author

A longtime FAA Designated Pilot Examiner and Accident Prevention Counselor, Howard Fried has administered practical tests to hundreds of aspiring pilots. During his career, he has logged an impressive 40,000-plus hours in many types of military and general-aviation aircraft. For the past 25 years, he has operated a flight school that trains pilots for all types of certifications and ratings. A member of the Lawyer Pilots Bar Association and writer, his entertaining columns are a popular feature of *Flying* magazine. He also lectures widely on aviation education and safety.